The Mushroom Girl

The Mushroom Girl

From Hitler's Germany to Today's Texas

Dagmar Grieder

Stoney Creek Publishing

Stoney Creek **Publishing**

A Member of the Texas Book Consortium

Published by

Stoney Creek Publishing Group

StoneyCreekPublishing.com

ISBN: 979-8-9879002-9-1
ISBN (ebook): 979-8-9879002-3-9
Library of Congress Control Number: 2024903532

Cover design by Market Your Industry, MarketYourIndustry.com

Contents

1. First Home

T his I believe: It is the role of the elders of the tribe to tell the stories of long ago.

I have been an elder or, to be politically correct, a senior citizen for some time now, taking advantage of discounts for movie tickets. I have not been much inclined, though, toward looking to the past. Then recently, a couple of things coincided, prompting me to think about my childhood during the rise and fall of Adolf Hitler's Third Reich. Except for a cousin in Poland, who is not inclined to reminisce, I am the oldest living person in my close family.

As I take up my pen, I realize that the decision to write these memories began with the death of Marian, my beloved first cousin, now a few years ago. He was the first of my generation, and though he died of natural causes, I sometimes wonder if the horrors he had to endure as a boy cut his life short. So, I try to rise to what seems almost an obligation. Describing the vignettes that stand out from my childhood and beyond in my memory is the easy part. The more difficult task is stringing them together into some sort of narrative. The pieces do not always fit together neatly. But the previous generation is all dead. I can no longer consult them for answers or clarifications. Imperfect though my recollections may be—as the line between remembering and remembering what we've been told blurs over time—I must chronicle the events of these tumultuous years as best I can. Since I am in the middle of my ninth decade, the time is surely now.

The things that I can remember are purely from my experiences of family life in turbulent times. Of the background, which is by far the more interesting, I had only a child's view. Even though I lived through them, I find that I know little about the sequence or extent of the events that reshaped Europe after almost destroying it. Modern European history, especially German history, was not taught in German schools after the Second World War when I was a student. Was it that we could not face what we had allowed to happen? I wonder if this period is taught in German schools even today, or has it been left to writers like Günter Grass to be the conscience of a whole nation and to atone for its—for our—collective guilt?

As I begin to write, it becomes apparent to me that, with all her faults and weaknesses, my mother emerges as the heroine of this piece. I am dedicating my effort to her memory.

I was born in the prestigious Women's Clinic in Gleiwitz, now Gliwize, Upper Silesia, and lived with my parents in the heavily industrialized city of Hindenburg, now Zabrze, in southwestern Poland. My father, Georg Josef Janiel, was a talented structural engineer and a successful businessman. When relatively young, he joined, as a junior partner, an established firm that designed and built steel structures below and above ground. In peacetime, that meant the construction of bridges and multistory buildings. Following a terrible depression, the company thrived in the economic boom of the late thirties and even more during the early years of the war. The firm expanded into areas required in the war effort, such as repairs not only on existing structures like bridges but also on tanks and locomotives. When my father's senior partner, his *compagnon*, wanted to retire, my father was prepared to buy him out.

My mother, Edeltraud Hildegard Janiel, nee Widawski, was his ten-years-younger trophy wife. While she certainly was not beautiful, she was pretty enough, sweet-natured, charming, and very elegant. Hospitality was and is a common value in the central and eastern parts of Europe, and my mother excelled in the art. She knew how to make a place inviting. People liked to visit, and she liked having guests. And, boy, could she cook and bake! She also had a beautiful singing voice and loved using it: to teach me children's songs and lullabies, to accompany the music from operettas and popular hits on the radio, to sing at family events.

I arrived five years into the marriage, on September 2, 1937, longingly awaited, especially by my mother, who suffered from feelings of inadequacy because of her barrenness, painful even more so after some relative on my father's side had said, in her hearing, that a tree that bore no fruit deserved to be pulled up and thrown away. She had had an earlier pregnancy, which had ended in a miscarriage with medical complications. At that time, the doctors told her it was unlikely that she could ever have children. My mother was the one to choose my name, and she was undecided. In the end, she put three slips of paper with her top choices into a flower vase and drew one. That is how I got my name, Dagmar, and it has served me well so far.

I was born small, less than six pounds, and had a hard time getting going. If my mother was disappointed that I was neither blond nor blue-eyed like her but looked more like a pale-skinned Roma foundling, she did not show it. Instead, she lavished love and care on me and dressed me up like a little princess. Although Hitler was already in power as the elected chancellor of Germany, World War II had not yet broken out. I would later brag that I was of good peacetime quality. The day before my second birthday, Hitler invaded Poland, and World War II began. There was no immediate impact. For the time being, life was still full of bliss.

One of my earliest memories is running naked through the house after my evening bath to find my father, my Papa, for his nightly ritual of taking me into his arms, patting me on my bottom, and calling me his little *Naktfrosch* (naked frog). But it was not the frog label that stuck as a nickname. Someone started calling me *Hasele* (little rabbit), a name that, to my great annoyance, family members used well into my school years. I seemed to be the center of the adults' attention in this well- regulated, privileged household and felt completely safe. My mother felt happy and protected. Her interests were centered on me and her family, not reaching further than the latest fashion coming out of Berlin, Vienna, and Prague, the cultural centers of our part of the world. About politics, she had no clue.

My father was more world-wise and skeptical about the truth of the propaganda that was spread by the government. He spoke Russian and a bit of English, and he followed the political news in the papers and on the radio, which included Hitler holding huge events and giving speeches that were broadcast over the entire country. He was also, at low volume, listening to foreign stations to hear the other side, an activity which was strictly *verboten*. I was used to being encouraged to talk and not to being shushed. To give my father a quiet house as he followed the news on radio, my mother had the bright idea to give me a bowl of dried peas and a bottle and a teaspoon, and she showed me how I could move the peas from one vessel to another, which kept me quiet and focused. This worked so well that she repeated it as needed and I came to associate the little game with speeches on the radio and urgently asked for peas every time somebody raised their voice on the "wireless." Even though he was skeptical about the truth of official state-managed news and about the outcome of the war, my father became a member of the National Socialist (Nazi) Party and wore the pin on the lapel of his suit. He was nonetheless dismissive about some of their activities. I think he was annoyed that the party expected him to participate in what he likely deemed a silly waste of his time.

I remember that once he came home with a metal cup the size and shape of a large beer stein, with a sealed lid and with a slit in its center into which one could drop a coin or insert a folded bill. He explained to me its use and I was quite interested, especially after he dropped a few coins into it from his pocket and it made a racket when I shook it. In the end, he gave me a few rolls of coins, and I delighted in feeding them one by one into the cup.

An important early memory is of a family outing in the country-side, where we loved to escape from the sooty and polluted air of Hindenburg for the fresh food that our hosts were happy to sell us. As usual, three generations of extended family gathered on that day, including my great uncle Max and his Ukrainian wife, Aunt Millie, pretty and cheerful with her dark curls and, frankly, quite fat. I don't think that she ever had any formal instruction in German, but she was not shy and was quite able to communicate, often making us laugh. She did not complain about the long walks, but hiking uphill was a challenge for her. To help, my uncle Hansi, my mom's fourteen-years-younger brother, and my oldest cousin, Marian, the two well known in the family as pranksters, would jump in, one taking Aunt Millie's hand and pulling her while the other pushed from her ample behind. In my mind's eye, aunt Millie is wearing a navy-blue silk dress with white polka dots, her favorite, which in her self-taught German she referred to as her *bepinkeltes* —"peed-on"— dress. She was a good sport about the laughter to which she gave rise. Now that walking uphill takes the stuffing out of me, I understand how she had to struggle on our extended walks through meadows and woods.

I must have been around four or five years old when, as we were taking one of those long walks, we came to a signpost that said,

"Stop! Do not go beyond this point! This is the border." (I think it was between Germany and Poland.) I could read a little, and it did not take long for me to understand what that meant. I remember tearing loose from my mother's hand and running past the sign, around it and back, my heart pounding. I had been abroad for the first time, the beginning of a lifelong fascination with foreign travel.

Another vacation with extended family comes to mind, this one in wintertime. Zakopane in the High Tatra Mountains is beautiful and popular all times of the year. The family photos show that my father was along, as were my Oma and Opa (grandma and grand-dad), my uncle Hansi, all three of my cousins with their mom, Aunt Mimi, and my Aunt Erna. We were in a nice resort. The paths had already been cleared of snow by the time we arrived, and the snow had been banked up on both sides of the path, taller than I. The cousins and uncle Hansi were on skis. My father and Aunt Erna pulled me on a toboggan, up a hill—there were no lifts—for a rush back down, with one of the adults sitting behind me. I remember my aunt Mimi teaching me how to make snow angels, and every now and then a spontaneous snowball fight would break out, all against all.

My brother was not yet born and maybe my mother was preg-nant with him, as she kept out of the fray and just walked sedately with her parents, she and Oma arm-in-arm, while the rest of us went crazy in the snow. She was not fond of such wild sport and preferred being dressed right for the occasion and looking elegant. I cringe while I write this: She was proudly wearing her mountain ocelot coat with matching hat. How could anyone, especially my animal-loving mother, wear a garment that had cost the lives of about a dozen of the rare and beautiful, and now endangered, spotted cats?

Alas, my enjoyment of the winter holiday came to a sudden halt when I fell sick with a virulent case of diarrhea. Imodium had not yet been invented. The only way to treat such a case was with diet and compressed charcoal tablets. Diet meant dry toast and tea, and not very much of that. Naturally, I had to stay in, and Oma sat with me, reading to me and entertaining me as best she could. I soon got hungry, but if my mother gave me even a tiny bit of what everybody else was eating, it went right through me.

I can still feel the pain it gave me to see food and to watch others enjoy theirs. To spare me this suffering, I was put to bed before the others had their evening meal. As I would lie listening to them talk and laugh and imagining them eating all kinds of delicacies, I became more and more self-pitying and resentful. I do not know whether tests ever revealed the source of my troubles or whether it became public knowledge that a period of freezing weather had broken some pipes in the resort and had compromised the purity of the water supply. We learned that typhus bacilli had invaded my digestive tract. My illness persisted even after we all returned to our homes, and I was then under the care of our family physician. He tried other diets and therapies. At one time, they even discussed blood transfusions from my own blood. Luckily, it did not come to that extreme therapy. As my mother gave me a little more solid food, the illness eventually ran its course, and it cured me of being a picky, poor eater. From then on, I had a healthy appetite—just as food became scarce.

Children in Germany, just as in America, are told that it is the stork that delivers babies. When my mother knew that she was pregnant again, she wisely decided to involve me. She gave me sugar cubes to put on the sooty windowsill before bedtime so that we might attract a stork. Later in the pregnancy, she let me put my ear on her growing belly to hear and feel the life within. So, finally, on July 2, 1942, when my little brother Michael was born, a few months before my fifth birthday, I had ownership in the event, and I remained my mother's partner throughout it. When my dad finally brought her and the new baby home from the hospital, she allowed me to watch Micky nurse, and even gave me a taste of what he was drinking, squeezing from her breast a few drops of milk onto a teaspoon. Micky, as some of us still call him today, was a nine-pounder, born somewhat bruised but with a little button nose and rolls of fat. My mother, showing him off to the family who visited her in the hospital, somewhat apologetically compared him to a little boxer. Unlike me, he had the nursing down pat from day one.

He cried so much and so fiercely that he suffered a hernia, and his navel, instead of looking like a dimple, stuck out like a little button. Slowly he outgrew these early difficulties, and in time some solid foods were added to his diet to keep him from crying so much. The mashed bananas that had been my snack when I was his age were no longer available. In their place Micky was offered, in his bottle, juice made from squeezing grated carrots through a napkin. That daily bottle of carrot juice gave his fat cheeks a golden glow. Everyone agreed he was extremely cute.

Both my little brother and I had the usual childhood illnesses. We passed through the chicken pox with little drama, but he was seriously sick when he came down with diphtheria. All I remember of his symptoms is a high fever against which baby aspirin was ineffective. I remember a few times he had to be wiped down with cool water and once even immersed and then wrapped into a wet sheet to bring down his temperature. In those days, the patient had to pass through what was called The Crisis, always happening during the night, with one or both parents stoically sitting by. The child would either survive the night and recover quickly or, in some sad cases, die. Micky lived.

Those times were BP, Before Penicillin, and there were several serious illnesses that were expectable encounters for most children, almost like rites of passage. I only know from being told that my first severe illness, which had to have included some pain, was a kidney infection when I was just a baby. I don't know how this was treated, but the after-effects would follow me into my teens because of my mother's now lifelong concern for my body's plumbing. "Don't sit on cold concrete." "Don't sit on this cold metal bench," and even more annoying, from school age on I was ordered to wear, over my ordinary panties so that I could not complain that they itched, a pair of woolen knickers, which went way down my thighs. "Just during the cold months," my mother assured me to counter my resistance. Of course, in Germany, that meant at least half of the year. Even though this loathsome garment was not visible under my skirts, I *knew* it was there, and I resented it and resented even more that my mother would lift the hem of my dress as I was trying to slip out the door, to make sure that I was in compliance.

A family photo shows me with a big scarf around my neck, and I remember being prone to sore throats so frequently that my parents discussed removing my tonsils. Luckily, it did not come to this, and I don't recall that either Micky or I had other serious illnesses until much later, when Micky, as a first or second grader, failed a school-wide test for tuberculosis. TB was rampant in Germany after the war when people did not have enough food and often lived in camps or other crowded circumstances. There was a stigma attached to TB as there was to syphilis, which was spread by the Russian occupying army. The spoils of war go to the winner, and the Russian soldiers claimed that "right" unchecked. Micky had an X-ray, in those days not an image but a visual exam by a trained X-ray technician that would have lasted several minutes. My mother was instructed to give him plenty of food and plenty of rest. The second was much easier than the first. It must have been a light case or a false diagnosis. No other therapy was ordered.

In 1942 and 1943, there was good news not only at home but, from the government's point of view, also on the national stage. By the time Micky was born, Hitler had advanced through Belgium and the Netherlands to France. A large part of that country, including Paris, had already been occupied for over a year. I have recently read that during this period, eighty-five percent of the food production of occupied France was diverted to Germany. Unfortunately, none of that wonderful food, for which France was and is so famous, made its way as far east as we lived.

By now, in addition to carrots for bananas, we had to get used to many other substitutions. The word *Ersatz* (substitute) still has seriously bad connotations in Germany. Germans had to settle for roasted barley in the place of coffee, margarine for butter, and potato starch for white flour. However, I don't believe that our family was yet short of food. My father proved to be a savvy provider. The shelves in the stores may have been bare, and everything was on ration cards anyway, but an under-the-counter market existed for those who could afford it. My father was genuinely interested in keeping his business connections well-polished, and he was a passionate angler. Factories typically had ponds on their terrains, and they stocked them with fish. So often when he had come home from a visit to a client or business associate, one or two fish would be swimming in the bathtub. This was no problem unless it was Saturday, the traditional day for tub baths in Europe in those days.

My father owned a multistory house on the so-called Ring, where the trolley tracks went around a central plaza in the middle of Hindenburg, our hometown, which was named for the German chancellor just before Hitler. However, we did not live in the multistory house but rented from Herr Bamberg, who lived downstairs, the upper floor of a villa in a ritzy neighborhood of luxury houses surrounded by lush gardens. A glass-enclosed veranda was a sweet place to gather and look down on Herr Bamberg's carefully tended flowers. When eggs became virtually unavailable, my crafty father had a coop and wire enclosure built in that large flower garden and installed some chickens there. Herr Bamberg was not at all happy to have his flower beds disturbed and argued that the chickens would attract flies, to which my clever father had a ready answer:

quite the contrary, chickens ate flies. He was a man used to getting his way.

Angela, our young Polish maid, announced that she, coming from the country, knew all there was to know about chickens, and she was now given, in addition to her household duties, the responsibility for the chickens' care. I don't want to speculate how she knew this, but every evening when she returned from closing the coop for the night, she would proudly give a forecast of the next day's number of eggs. These birds were purely utilitarian, not pets like the purebred exotic and heritage chickens I now keep in my yard. We never gave them names, nor did we attempt to form a bond with them. I remember being deeply resentful when our lone goose once painfully pinched my tummy when I trailed after Angela as she tended to the poultry. With hindsight, I cannot say that I blame the goose. My parents had sinister plans for her.

Angela must have been homesick. From her stories, I created in my imagination a magical place as her village. After much pleading, I was once allowed to go with her on one of her visits home, and I remember I found everything about this visit disappointing, especially the chimney-sweep flowers she had often talked about, which had blossomed in my mind's eye into large roses like the crepe-paper flowers that my Aunt Erna was so skilled in winning for me at carnival shooting galleries. I imagined them in a luscious, dark chocolate brown. They turned out to be only a modest type of grass with a little blackish tuft, an early lesson in skepticism for me.

Angela had learned during her growing-up years in a village how to fatten a goose for the special holiday dinner, when it would be roasted to crispy, golden perfection. She did this job in our kitchen, sitting on a low stool, holding the doomed creature firmly between her sturdy knees. One-by-one, she force-fed the goose a bowl full of some kind of long dumplings, which she had prepared in advance for this procedure. With her left hand she opened the beak and held it that way, pinching from both sides. With her right hand, she dropped a dumpling into the wide-open beak and with her index finger she gave it a little shove. Then she allowed the goose to close its mouth and, holding the head high to keep the long neck extended, she stroked it with the fingers of her right hand, moving the lump down its length until the bulge disappeared into the goose's body. She would keep doing this until the bowl was empty. Apparently, all this was done with the enthusiastic approval of my otherwise tender-hearted mother. It probably also was Angela's duty to dispatch, eviscerate, and pluck the goose when the appointed day arrived, but I was carefully shielded and never had to witness it. Likely this was done while I napped or after my bedtime. My mother was a splendid cook and a master at roasting geese. To this day, roast goose, with the traditional sides of red cabbage and potato dumplings, ranks high among the tastiest meals in my life.

While Angela had experience in fattening and butchering geese, it was my father, the angler himself, who was in charge of dispatching the fish he brought home. From these events I was also carefully, and with much drama on her part, shielded by my mother. She would take me into my parents' bedroom and into the large marital bed, where she hugged me tightly, with both of our heads buried into the huge feather pillows. Thus, we could comfort each other until my father came into the room to announce that it was safe to come out again. Often the fish was a carp, not particularly delicious and with many bones. Sometimes we got lucky and it was trout, and my father loved to have it baked in the oven. A trout prepared this way was called "blue. "My mother, who had once had food poisoning from a meal of fish, had a lifelong dislike for it, and I can imagine that it was difficult for her to overcome her disgust and prepare the fish for my father's dinner.

To my mother's great sorrow, I was a poor eater and stayed small and skinny. The more she fretted, the more I liked the attention and soon saw this as my role in the daily family drama. When cod liver oil and "Pepsin" failed to stimulate my appetite, a plan to use psychology was devised: the child of one of my father's workers was invited to come to our house every noon to eat lunch with me. This experiment was successful, at least for the little girl, who would first eat her meal and then finish mine.

With Micky in his large pram, my parents would take us on walks into the euphemistically called "fresh air" of our coal-driven industrial town. There was so much soot in the air that windowsills had to be washed regularly and the rag was always black. Often our destination was a large park called St. Guido Woods, where regional wild animals were kept in fenced pastures and pens. I remember deer, foxes, and, my favorites, raccoons. They are called "wash bears" in German, for their habit of dunking everything into water before they devour it. Little did I know how fierce and destructive these creatures can be and how deadly a threat to chickens, and that I would later, in Texas, chase them out of our very own screened porch. But back then, I thought they were adorable.

I clearly remember that on some of these walks we came past a midden, where people had dumped worn-out items like bicycles and household goods. There, even though I was not yet school age, a lifelong passion for recycling materials and a horror of throwing things away made its early appearance. I always saw things on that pile that seemed perfectly useful to me and that I wanted to take home. I distinctly remember one white enameled washbasin, which, though chipped, still seemed to me to have a lot of life left. My parents had to appease me by assuring me we would pick these items up on our way home, and then they had to choose a circuitous route, avoiding the midden on the return home. Today it is fashionable to recycle and be green. I was just an early advocate.

I don't recall ever going to kindergarten, but I do remember getting ready for first grade. It had to be 1943. I was eager to go to school and to learn how to read better and to start writing. On the first day of school, it was the custom then to give the new pupil a

Schultüte, a large cone made of colorful stiff paper that was filled with goodies: crayons, pencils, erasers, but also apples, cookies, candy, whatever treat could be found in those days of scarcity. Since paper was difficult to find, we first-graders all wrote on slates with a stylus. I remember little about school except that the brainwashing started early. We greeted our teacher with "Heil Hitler" in the morning and were told stories and shown film clips that documented how much the *Führer* (leader), loved little kids, who loved him in return and would bring him flowers whenever he was at a gathering, receiving the adoration of a crowd.

We also drilled marching down into our school's basement whenever the sirens sounded an alarm, something that started happening more and more often. Air raids were not just signaled during the day. They also happened during the night. There was a procedure that we had to follow. Most important, all windows had to be darkened during the night, and wardens patrolled the neighborhood to make sure that no cracks let light out to provide enemy planes with a target. In our house, the basement was outfitted to serve as an air-raid shelter. There were some very basic provisions: water, a first aid kit and a bucket of sand, presumably to put out a fire if needed. There had to be something for us to sit on. My father would take me by the hand and my mother would lift the sleeping baby Micky out of his crib, and we would all march down to the basement. My mother would insist that we all huddle together. After the sirens blew the "all clear" we would go back upstairs, and if it was night, we would go back into our beds and try to fall asleep again. During the day, I would ask permission after the raid to go outside and look for bomb shrapnel. My cousins, of whom you will read more, had planted this idea in my head by showing me their growing collections. They traded with other kids the way American kids trade baseball cards and they generously gave me a couple of little pieces. Since the area where I was permitted to look was basically just our front yard, I was always disappointed. No bombs ever fell in our quiet little neighborhood.

I don't know where my cousins got their bomb shrapnel, but I adored and admired them, and everything they said and did seemed exciting to me. At one visit they declared that they had founded a club, the *Adlerverein,* Eagle Club, of which they generously let me be an honorary member. I was much chagrined that they were allowed to do things that I was not permitted to do. For instance, they had permission to pitch a tent in the back yard and sleep in it during the night. Even though I begged and begged, and they declared that they would protect me, my parents were united in their decision and did not permit it.

I loved our visits at my cousins' home in Nicolai, possibly named for the last Russian Tsar Nicolas. It must have been a small town or village. I cannot find it on any map, old or new. Their house with its big yard and orchard backed onto fields of grain and potatoes. With my cousins as my guides, we roamed in those fields. I remember that after the cutting of the grain the plants were bundled, and several bundles were stood up leaning against each other to let the ears dry. My cousins claimed, and delivered proof by tipping some of these pyramids, that they could find the nests of live mice. I had never in my life seen a live mouse and certainly had not seen little mouse babies. They also knew that after a field of potatoes had been dug up and harvested, if one looked hard enough, one could find the occasional potato that had been missed. At the end of the potato harvest the farmers would gather all the pulled-up plants, pile them up and set them on fire for ashes with which to fertilize the field for the next year's crop. When we got lucky and found some potatoes, we would push them into the fire with a stick and later find them all charred on the outside, with delicious, smoky-tasting potato pulp inside. This was also a place where, in season, we were given delicious fruit from Aunt Mimi's and Uncle Emil's own orchard. The only difficult part was the strictly observed rule that you could not drink water for a whole hour after eating fresh fruit, which meant of course that as soon as we had finished eating our treat, we became intolerably thirsty.

My cousins were not just experts on shrapnel, they also knew how to identify airplanes that would occasionally fly over the area. There never was any bombing; there was just not a worthy target. Nevertheless, my cousins would teach me how to dive into the ditch along the road when they identified an approaching formation of planes as American. They were less worried about the "Russkies," who they claimed were not good at hitting targets. As the war effort became more desperate, probably in 1943 or 1944, the two older boys, Marian and Felix, had to join and attend meetings of the Hitler Youth, sort of like Boy Scouts but with a heavy emphasis on Nazi propaganda. My uncle Hansi, about eighteen years old, had already been drafted into the military. Marian, the oldest, maybe fifteen by then, was forced to join a defense team in which he and the other boys his age were trained to operate an anti-aircraft weapon, called *Flack*. This worried his mother, my aunt Mimi, to no end, as such installations would be considered primary targets by the Allied Air teams. Marian was not allowed to leave his station. He would have been shot like any adult soldier for deserting. He was a good-looking young man, and my desperate aunt Mimi even schemed that she might smuggle girl's clothes to him and help him get away disguised as a woman.

I recently celebrated my eighty-fifth birthday, and I can still get excited about birthdays. I remember them as grand occasions with family and friends gathered all around. These events were carefully planned, with a well-considered guest list. For the party the honoree's chair would be decorated with garlands of greenery and flowers. Little place cards drawn by my mother, who had a knack for making cute drawings, assured that everybody was seated at their proper place. Poems were composed and recited, and songs were sung for the honoree. I was no more than three years old when, for my father's birthday, my mother helped me to memorize a little poem she had written. `

> Mein liebes, gutes Papilein (*My dear, good Daddy*)
> Ist das Häschen noch so klein (*However small the little Rabbit is,*)
> So liebt es dich doch inniglich (*She loves you dearly*)
> Der liebe Gott beschütze dich (*May God protect you*)

Lifted onto a dining chair, I recited the poem for him and his guests to gentle applause. Before I could be lifted off the chair, I announced that I knew another poem and recited a naughty, two-line zinger that my Aunt Erna had secretly taught me. This brought down the house, and I was swiftly returned to the *Kinderzimmer* (children's room) and the tender care of Angela before I could get into more mischief.

For my own birthdays, which I naturally remember best, there were singing and dancing and games and of course cake and candles and place cards and party favors and lots of guests. From my father's side came my grandparents and my Aunt Lucy with her children, my cousins: Edgar, a little older than I, Marlies, about my age, and little Tessa, a couple of years younger. Their father, my father's brother, had been inducted into the military early on and was soon killed in battle, the first casualty of the war in our inner circle. There was also Peter, with his mother, who may have been the token "poor" relatives. Peter was a shy and quiet boy, who for reasons I do not know did not have a father. The visitors from my mother's side were my grandparents, Oma and Opa, and my mother's sister, Aunt Mimi, with her husband, Uncle Emil. He was still young but already bald. Their sons, Jurek, Felix, and Marian, were my beloved cousins, two, five, and eight years older than I, respectively. Also present was my Uncle Hansi, mother's fourteen-years-younger brother and only a couple of years older than his nephew Marian. The two behaved more like cousins, were funny and often surprised the family with elaborate tricks. I remember one visit when a thunderstorm dumped a lot of rain on us. We scrambled for umbrellas that were there for our convenience, only to find out that the rods had been replaced by lengths of rubber pipe by the two pranksters, which made them useless as protection from rain.

Finally, also invited to my birthday parties was Babette, my little day-to-day best friend, who lived in the villa across the street. Some thirty years later, when Americans suddenly became curious about their roots, I did, too. I decided to make a visit to my family and to the region of my childhood, which was now again a part of Poland. (When World War II ended with the defeat of Germany, large parts of Europe were divided up by the Allied leaders, Churchill, Roosevelt, Stalin, and de Gaulle, in the famous conference at Yalta.) My cousins took turns being my guides, doubling up as their schedules allowed. Among other meaningful places they took me to the house where I had lived as a child. We approached on a tree-lined street that I remembered well. I had often walked it with my mother on her errands. The trees were maples, and in the early summer I could find some of their "blooms" on the ground, little pockets for the growing seed with a wing attached. I could open the little pocket, remove the seed and spread out the sticky pocket and stick it on my nose. When we came close to our destination, we saw two little girls playing with a doll buggy, and I had the weird feeling that I was seeing Babette and myself some thirty years ago. The house was much smaller than in my memory, and the formerly white stucco walls were now almost black with soot. As we were standing across the street, a woman arrived on a bicycle. She looked suspiciously at us, and one of my cousins explained to her in Polish that I had lived there as a child. Without a word she entered the house, slamming the door behind her and shattering my hope that I might be allowed to peek inside. The moment I had arrived from Germany my cousins urged me to speak only English, never German, when we were in public places, even in the staircase of their apartment building. The well-justified resentments against Germans in general were still fresh and raw.

An important member of the family who was always present at family celebrations was my Aunt Erna. She was not a blood relative but both my and my brother's godmother. I was later told that my father boycotted our christenings. He had, by that time, officially left the Roman Catholic Church, as many others had, either for business or Nazi party reasons or because he was too stingy to pay church taxes. Aunt Erna was my mother's best friend from their days together as teenagers in a finishing school in an Ursuline cloister, where, apparently, she had been the terror of the poor nuns. She smoked and drank from an early age and her escapades were legendary, providing stories throughout our growing-up years.

Aunt Erna would become even more important to us at and after the end of the war, as you will soon learn. She was a petite and good-looking young woman with an enterprising spirit and boundless energy, beloved by all for her generosity and her great sense of humor. She was not a girly girl. As I remember, she favored tailored clothes, fedora hats, and suits with skirts and sometimes pants, hardly ever worn by women in those days except for snow sports during winter. She had been engaged to marry once, but the wedding was, at the last moment, called off for reasons I never knew. Her parents, no doubt relieved that their unconventional daughter was going to be domesticated after all, had spent a great deal of money on a trousseau. I believe that in today's more tolerant environment, she might have chosen to live as a lesbian. I remember she owned only one single dress, one that my mother had sewn for her.

I remember little about my paternal grandparents. My mother

gave preference to the distaff side of the family. I recall that my paternal granddad, my Opa, Julius Janiel, owned and managed a fancy resort of some kind in Beuthen, some distance away, that included inside and garden dining and boasted an indoor swimming pool, a rarity in those days. Maybe they visited less often because it was harder for them to be away. His wife, Maria, my paternal Oma, was a sweet woman who liked to stay in the background.

I know much more about my maternal grandparents. My Oma Elisabeth, from whom I get my middle name, was tall, slender, and erect well into old age. She was not conventionally pretty, but elegant and well groomed. She was also vain, especially about her beautiful blond and later silver hair. Oma was loving to me and Micky and very patient when one of us was sick. Later, when I was in my mid-teens, she came to visit us for a couple of weeks in West Germany. I guiltily remember that I was feeling resentful: she slept with my hair curlers every single night of her stay. That was the last time I saw her until I was in my mid-thirties.

My maternal grandfather was the interesting one. My cousins and I called him Opa, but all others referred to him as "Tate," pronounced tah-teh. I do not know whether he was an engineer, or chemist, or businessman, but at some time in the nineteen teens he went to Russia to function as the director, we would say CEO, of a factory that produced enamelware. It was in or near Ekaterinburg, not far from the Ural River. I assume this was to be for an extended period, as he took his wife and two grade-school-aged daughters with him. I think I must have inherited his curiosity about exotic lands and people.

My mother liked stories and was very good at telling them. On some weekend mornings, when we were not in a hurry to get dressed and going, we loved to get into bed with her, sitting at the foot end, under her covers. The stories she told about this period of her life were my favorites. How I wish I could ask her now about timing and details, which I was too young or too thoughtless to question when I still could. How do I reconcile my grandfather's going to Russia with the First World War? Maybe they left from Poland, not Germany. My mother told me about her best friend there, Myriam, the child of a Tatar family, Muslims, who ate strange food, wore different clothes, and had a different way of praying, who in the hot part of the year would sleep on cots on their house's flat roof.

My grandfather's job came with a house surrounded by a large garden and a story. We were told that the previous director's wife had been murdered by a mob, who pulled her out of the house by her long hair and drowned her in the fountain. Since her death the house was said to be haunted. My grandparents apparently became acquainted with other Europeans with whom they socialized. Occultism was all the rage then, and my grandfather engaged a medium, who on at least one occasion held a séance, during which all present were instructed to lay their hands flat on the tabletop before them and then raise their hands together, and lo and behold, the table rose and lifted off the floor. At that gathering or others they heard a noise from the ceiling as though horses and riders were galloping through the attic. As best I can figure, my mother was then about seven years old and Mimi, her sister, nine. The séance would undoubtedly have been held after their bedtime. So from whom did my mother learn the details of that evening? I heard these stories many times over the years, and my mother never wavered about the details but spoke with great conviction.

My mother also told a story about Mimi, Myriam and herself, she the youngest of the three, exploring the area and coming to the banks of a creek or river. So was this the mighty Ural or a small tributary, who knows? They came across a woman who was washing clothes in the river water when some mess, including an air-filled bubble, came floating along, probably the intestines and bladder of a slaughtered animal. My mother asked the woman what it was, and the woman said: "Why, this is a human egg." Later my mother was embarrassed when, back in Europe and in school, she told at show-and-tell that she had seen a human egg floating along in the water in Russia, and she was thoroughly laughed at.

I do not know how long my family stayed in Russia, but I can make a fair guess what put an end to it: the Bolshevik Revolution. My grandfather put my Oma and the girls onto a train home while he stayed behind to oversee an orderly transfer of his duties, most likely to the Bolshevik government. But where was home? Was it the little house surrounded by a beautiful garden that I remember, where in the summer Opa fed us children sweet, juicy pears from a tree that he had scaffolded onto the sunny side of the house? I have many more questions I would like to ask: In what language did my mother speak with Myriam, in what language did she address the laundering woman, and how did the woman answer? I know from my own experience that as a child one can quickly learn. I, at the age of about eight, in a short time and without a single hour of formal teaching, learned enough Czech to play with the children of the new owner of the house and bakery, to attend second grade in Czech school, and to translate for my mother when she had the occasional opportunity to buy a black market smoked cheese from a peasant woman selling out of a basket at a street corner.

The train trip from Russia lasted several days and nights and was not very comfortable. My mother said that both she and her sister disliked using the bathroom when everything was in motion. She told me that their mother, my Oma, had a large bottle of cologne, which she used for freshening up the sisters and herself. Once when she was doing that, a Russian man came down the aisle between the seats and, exclaiming that this was a horrible waste, ripped the bottle out of her hands and drank the rest.

When I remember visits to my grandparents, my grandfather seems to have already been retired, because he was always at home. He still liked to smoke a fine cigar and drink a glass of champagne.

He loved classical music and hated drafts, like most Europeans. He used to play the piano for us, eventually getting teary-eyed, exhorting us to be thankful for being together, since this might be the last time we had the chance. Alas, the day came when he was right. Did he have premonitions or symptoms of illness that he had not revealed? He died after a short battle with throat cancer before the end of the war. I do the math: if Mimi was about ten or eleven at the time in Russia, and he had become a father around thirty, he must have been born around 1880. That means he died in his early or mid-sixties. In those days a cancer diagnosis was a death sentence. My mother had a strange experience. She dreamed that there was a lit candle, and she was told or just understood that she needed to keep it burning, even though it was windy. She tried to shelter the flame with her hands, but try as she might, the light was blown out, and she woke up. The next morning the phone call came that her father had died during the night.

Easter is about a month away as I write this. It was not just my family that celebrated holy days. I believe that most Europeans like to mark the special days on the calendar. Of course, Easter was a day of feasting, but I cannot be sure that I remember that special meals were associated with the celebration; maybe a ham baked in a bread crust. Yes, eggs were hard-boiled and painted, and during the war years they were scarce and therefore special. Everybody was glad to get some. Chocolate bunnies were unavailable.

There was a special Easter rite that I have not encountered outside the area where I lived as a child, now a part of Poland and the Czech Republic. As best I remember the men and boys had saplings from a willow tree or even a kind of whip braided from such willow saplings with which they would whip girls and each other gently, and females and males of all ages had little bottles of water, sometimes scented with a dash of cologne, that they would use to sprinkle each other. You might guess that such a custom can easily get out of control because of high-jinks or maybe because of the chance to settle some small score. It did occasionally happen that somebody was awakened by getting smacked a little too painfully or doused with cold water while still in bed.

The highlight in the ritual calendar of my childhood was Christmas. On December 6, St. Nikolaus ushered in the season along with his rough servant Ruprecht in a kind of good-cop, bad-cop routine. He would bring goodies to the nice children, while Ruprecht would bring coals to the naughty ones. Like every other child in Germany, I put my shoes, not my stockings, outside the door to my room at bedtime. I would jump out of bed the following morning to see what had been deposited in them. Usually, I got an apple and maybe some nuts in one shoe and, to keep me on the straight and narrow, a couple of pieces of coal in the other.

About this time, the Advent Wreath would appear floating over the center of our dining table, suspended on four strands of red ribbon from a red-painted wooden stand with a gold star on the top. On the fat circle of fir foliage stood four red candles; we lit the first one on the Sunday four weeks before Holy Night and an additional one each Sunday following, until all four were burning just before Christmas. Another way to prepare for and anticipate this greatest of holidays was the Advent Calendar. It covered the time from December 1 till December 24, Christmas Eve. It typically was the picture of a Christmas scene, usually with a kind of barn in the center. And there were numbered little doors, one to be opened each day until Holy Night. I was allowed to open the daily little door, which would show something Christmasy until finally the big door would reveal the holy parents with baby Jesus.

During those last few days before Christmas, the French doors to the dining room would be conspicuously shut, and secret proceedings went on behind them. Now my parents took their evening meal on a small table in our *Herrenzimmer* (gentlemen's room) as we called our living room, maybe harking back to the days when men's and women's quarters were segregated, as they still are in some Muslim countries. On Christmas Eve, after our meal of fish soup or baked carp, the doors to the dining room were finally opened. In the corner, usually occupied by a spindly rubber tree plant, the tall Christmas tree was decorated with heirloom blown-glass ornaments and white burning candles that filled the room with golden light and with the honey smell of the melting beeswax.

The effect was magical. No diving under the tree where the gifts lay; we would stand around the tree, together singing Christmas carols, not only German ones but also the hauntingly beautiful Polish songs of my mother's own childhood. I cannot remember many Christmases without some little twig getting singed or even catching fire, which added a crackling sound and the delicious scent of burning conifer to the festive aroma. These accidental fires were quickly extinguished with little alarm. There was no real danger, as the candles were not let burn for long, and the tree was never unattended. Finally, the candles were snuffed out, and we could now turn our attention to the gifts which the Christ child (*Christkind*), not Santa Claus, had brought. I remember my gifts being modest and becoming more so as scarcity set in. I would get books and dolls that were already mine and had disappeared without my having noticed. Now they were here again, spruced up, repaired and dressed up in new clothes that were often tiny copies of my own outfits.

For such festive occasions, it was not enough to deck me out in my best finery. My mother felt she had to do something about my uncooperative hair, which she complained grew as straight as chives. This was to be improved with the help of a metal curling iron, which she would heat in the kitchen over a flame on her gas stove. When it started glowing red, she tested its temperature on a piece of newspaper, and the kitchen promptly filled with acrid smoke. Then she let the iron cool a little before trying to curl under the straight-cut bottom of my chin-length hair. I, always worried that she would burn me, fidgeted and twitched. Consequently, I was always burned a little, but never seriously enough for my mother to give up on that idea.

There was a lot of visiting back and forth between the different parts of the family, often by train when my father could not come along because of business commitments. I remember watching the landscape stream by through the train window during the day and the moon accompany our route in the dark. I would practice my ABCs by writing them with my finger onto the fogged-up window of the overheated carriage. I have a distinct and painful memory of one such trip: in a station in the corner of one of the loading platforms, there was a crowd of people huddled together with a little bit of luggage. They were being guarded by armed soldiers or police with large dogs. I had never seen people with such strange clothes and hairstyles. I can still see in my mind's eye a girl, a little older than I, whose hair was parted sideways across the top of her head from ear-to-ear and then braided into an upper and a lower braid. Even though I was a small child, I understood they were hungry and in some terrible trouble. I asked my mother if we could give them some food out of the basket which we always brought with us, but she told me that, unfortunately, that was strictly *verboten* and that it was rude of me to stare.

It must have been the time when all of Germany's population had been processed and classified into ethnic groups. Thanks to my father's completely German family tree, we all were *Volksgruppe* (ethnic group) I, but my poor Oma and Opa, whose last name, Widawski, was a dead giveaway of their mixed German-Polish bloodlines (my Oma's maiden name had been Petrushka, the Polish word for parsley), were classified Group III. This worried my mother to no end. In the evenings, my parents held whispered conversations and even I understood that certain acquaintances of theirs, indeed whole families, were disappearing. Some had been able to leave the country, but others chose suicide as the only way out. It was a miserable time for people to be Jewish. If they were in government service, they had been dismissed or demoted. Their businesses had been vandalized, and every Jewish adult now had to wear a six-pointed yellow star stitched on their outer clothing.

Hitler, in power before my birth and before the beginning of the war, was very popular throughout Germany through the early war years for creating plentiful good jobs through huge public works projects such as the building of the *Autobahn,* still the backbone of the German road system. He did get the economy going and finally pulled Germany out of the terrible depression when inflation had risen exponentially. During that period, the currency lost value faster than new bills could be printed, and extra sets of zeros were simply stamped onto the bills to turn thousands into millions and millions into billions. There are stories that people needed wheelbarrows to take money to the bakery for a loaf of bread. Much later, when, in Austin, I was the manager of a local bank's international services department, folks would come in with shoe boxes full of such German bank notes and were very disappointed when I had to tell them that this currency was indeed interesting but unfortunately had no value.

A generation of grateful Germans picked up on the idea of a master race and would give their children names that harked back to the heroes and heroines of the Germanic sagas, in which Hitler had created a renewed interest. There are few Johns and Marias among my contemporaries in Germany, but a lot of Siegfrieds, Helgas, Gudruns, and Brunhilds.

When Hitler annexed Austria in 1939 to give the burgeoning German population more space to live, *Lebensraum,* Austrians greeted his armies with flowers and jubilation. Six years later, when the war ended with Germany's loss and our occupation by the Allied Forces, not a single Austrian seemed to remember this. German expansion into Czechoslovakia and Poland came next. In the negotiated "Munich Agreement" Czechoslovakia, outnumbered and out-armed, accepted Germany's annexation of

"Sudetenland" a region in the country's west, populated mostly by ethnic Germans. On September 1, 1939, Hitler invaded Poland. In response, France and England declared war on Germany, but there were no hostilities for two years. In both Poland and Czechoslovakia, the resistance organized underground, while Hitler tore at the social fabric by marking Jews and other minorities "undesirables and harmful" and moving them forcibly into ghettos and concentration camps.

While spirits were high after the early advances of the army of the Third Reich, by 1943 or 1944, the mood was turning bleak. It was too dangerous to mention any criticism out loud or make defeatist remarks. The German radio newscasts and weekly movie newsreels now focused only on the number of enemy planes and ships destroyed. They gave a rosy spin to the events, exhorting the population to conserve resources and sacrifice for the war. They promised a turnaround and certain ultimate victory for Germany through the imminent introduction of the new V-weapons, "wonder weapons." It was now dangerous, considered treason, to listen to foreign news, and it is a good thing my father, who spoke not only Russian but also English, was never caught with his ear cocked to the turned-low BBC on our *Volksempfänger* (peoples' receiver radio) in the evenings.

Even during these hard times, our family retained some of our old lifestyle. Before the arrival of children, my parents had traveled as a couple to the grand cities of Central and Eastern Europe: Vienna, Salzburg, Prague, Munich, Berlin, for world-class cultural events and fancy shopping. After we were born, the destinations became more child friendly. Our city was very sooty because of all the coal mining and heavy industry. So, during the summer, every year, the extended family on my mother's side would congregate in a village by the name of Lipowiez, which my Aunt Mimi had scouted out. Today, I cannot find Lipowiez on any map. It may be too small, or it may no longer exist. Judging from the name and the fact that the locals spoke Polish, I must assume that it was in already-occupied Poland. Once there, the inner circle of our family always lodged in the same farmhouse of an older couple. Gospodash and Gosposha (master and mistress), as we called our hosts, had a couple of grown sons and at least one unmarried adult daughter. That we were so enthusiastically welcomed there may have been because my mother and Aunt Mimi, and certainly my Oma, spoke Polish as well as they did German.

Also, when we came, we always brought presents from the city. I remember one of these gifts very well. It was a false braid for the daughter. On Sundays, the devoutly Catholic country people would dress up for church services in elaborate regional costume: white blouse with big lacy puff sleeves, black velvet bodice, full hand-woven wool skirt and an embroidered half apron. The complete costume was very valuable and weighed at least ten to fifteen pounds. All the women of the village wore the same outfit, just different colors and more or less elaborate depending on the wealth of the family. One could identify other villages by slight variations in the components. From the day of our gift onward, for dress-up, the fat false braid we had given the daughter would hang down her back under her kerchief, all the way to her waist. I hope it accomplished its purpose and helped her to find a good husband.

In this village, we would spend our entire days outside breathing the fresh, clean air of the countryside. We children, those of us less than school age and naked as jaybirds, would run around like little Indians, rolling down the grassy slopes, piling up rocks, digging in the bank or splashing in the Vistula (or maybe it was one of its tributaries). The women sat under the shade of some willow trees, reading or doing needlework, and would, without distinction, hug, kiss, feed or wipe off any child as necessary, just like a colony of monkeys. The men who were there (my father was often absent for reasons of work) would carve little boats for us children out of thick pieces of tree bark or make whistles from a piece of willow branch. They also tried to catch fish with their bare hands in the dark water under the grassy edges of the banks. In the evenings, men and boys went out with lanterns and flashlights to catch baskets and buckets full of crayfish, which I remember being the size of small lobsters. The following day, these would be boiled until they turned bright red and then consumed in a communal outdoor meal, accompanied by fruit and cakes, which had been lowered into the well on ropes to cool.

As the only girl among the children, I was protected and pampered. My Aunt Mimi, the mother of three boys, loved me especially well. I was the daughter she could not have. Every day she would string together little daisies into a fresh circlet of flowers for my hair, and while I was still little, that was all I wore. But being the only girl, and being little, also had its disadvantages, as in my not being allowed to spend the night in my cousins' makeshift tent.

.When I was seven years old and should have gone to second grade, we were often sent home early. School would soon be discontinued because of the frequent bomb raids, or else my parents just stopped sending me. The sirens would now sound the alarm during the day and night, sending all of us to the cellar bomb shelter, where my mother would hold her arms around us so that if anything happened to one, it would happen to all.

This had to be the time when my father, who had escaped the draft until now because his business was so important to the war effort, was called up. I remember crying and crying and my teacher consoling me, exhorting me to be thankful and proud that he had the chance to support the *Führer* and to protect us from bad enemies. My father was the last of his generation in the family to be drafted. The first had been his brother, my uncle Ernst, who had fallen. Then Uncle Hansi, not yet twenty, had received the dreaded summons.

There are two versions in the family lore explaining why my father had finally been called up.

I had always assumed that it was because the German military, by that time, was simply running too low on men to consider any extenuating factors. My cousin Marian, much later, showed me a very different scenario: my father, for reasons of self-protection or self-interest, had joined first the National Socialist Party and maybe later even the SS. In one or the other capacity, he had been required to witness the hanging of several Jewish people. My father, according to Marian, was so affected by the experience that he became ill and vomited in public.

Again, according to Marian, his summons arrived within days. He came home for only one brief visit as a soldier. I imagine it was at the end of some very basic training and before deployment to the Eastern front. To this day I cannot understand why he would choose me, a child, to tell that during an inspection the pocket of his uniform shirt was only partly buttoned, and he, who was used to giving the orders, was publicly chastised by his drill sergeant for being "half-dressed." It would be a long time before we saw him again or even knew that he was alive. Many families had been separated as we had been by circumstances beyond our control and locating one another was difficult. Then, if you walked through any park or public place with trees, the trunks would be completely covered with little notes giving the name of the person seeking, the name of the person sought, and a place to meet. It took my father some four years to locate us. With the help of the Red Cross and the radio search service, which at certain times during the day would broadcast the names of persons searching for their relatives, he finally located my mother and wrote her a letter. By this time, the winds of war had blown my parents in different directions. With a certain amount of acrimony on both sides, the marriage ended in divorce. But I am getting ahead of myself.

With my father drafted, my mother was left alone in the house with little Micky and me and our maid, Angela. Angela had been with us since she was seventeen years old. The poor girl must have missed her family and friends, as she was always telling me in glowing colors about her life among them. My mother, not that much older than she, treated her more like a younger friend or relative, teaching her to cook, embroider, and knit. I also remember that my mother took a keen interest in Angela's adventures with the opposite sex on her occasional days or evenings off. I believe that my mother, even after her marriage, missed romance in her life.

2. Fleeing from the Russians

Now, with my father away at the front, we had none of the food he had been so skillfully providing us. My poor mother and Angela could barely cope with the long waits in line for groceries. There were ever-increasing bomb raids and mounting fear of the advancing Russian armies, whose shelling could now be heard daily in our city. One day, my mother came home from an errand and was sobbing. She had been walking past a bombed site where, behind barbed wire and under armed guard, some Russian prisoners of war were clearing rubble. They stopped their work for a moment when they saw her pass by and one of them, grinning, drew his forefinger across his throat in a gesture for which there could only be one interpretation.

In tears and almost hysterical, my mother called my Aunt Erna, who arrived the next day. After much discussion deep into the night, the two decided that we should all go to stay for a while with Aunt Erna's parents, who lived farther west in Jägerndorf (now Krnov), a town in the hilly region of Sudetenland, the area of Czechoslovakia the Third Reich annexed in 1939. Aunt Erna's father was a master baker with a large bakery and bake shop in the center of town. Not only would we be safer farther west and therefore farther from the Russian front, but also, with plenty of bread and other baked products, there would always be enough to eat. While the two young women began to pack, Angela was told to wrap the best paintings, the best silver and the most valuable carpets in paper and haul them down to the cellar. She was made to stack them up in a corner and was told to shovel the mountain of coal, there as winter fuel, over the stash to conceal it until we could return. No one thought that we were leaving forever. That was unimaginable. I was told that I could take one single toy with me, and I still remember agonizing over the selection. I tried to cheat, and in the end my mother chose the expensive doll, *Rosenrot* (Rosy Red), which I finally took with me—a doll I still possess. Along with food for the journey and some changes of clothes, my mother and Aunt Erna also packed my mother's jewelry, my father's Leica camera, a set of silver flatware for each of us, and the last pages of the bank books and account statements that showed ending balances. During her entire life, my mother loved beautiful clothes. I can still see her in my mind with perfect clarity today, wearing several of her designer outfits. The memory is clear enough that I could render them in great detail. Among them was an elegant, black wool suit with silver fox trim, and, of course, her spotted ocelot coat could not be left behind.

My parents' sedan had long been requisitioned by the army of the Third Reich. Before our luggage could be fully loaded onto my father's delivery truck, the military confiscated that, too. So the suitcases were piled into the sidecar of my father's motorcycle, and either my Aunt Erna or the young Angela drove it to the railroad station. The rest of us had to walk. Micky, now out of his pram, was pushed in his foldable stroller. It had to be the winter of 1944. Little Micky's red nose and cheeks alone peered out from a fur sack —blue cloth on the outside and white sheepskin on the inside—that kept him warm. The sack lined the stroller and had a built-in muff inside to protect his little paws from the grim cold. This fur sack would years later get a second life as a snappy Ike-style jacket for me, stitched together by my clever mother's skilled hands, with a fat red zipper down the front and red knitted cuffs and collar.

At the train station we found chaos. People were everywhere, some sitting or sleeping on their luggage. Trains were only going in one direction, west, away from the advancing Russian front, and they no longer followed any schedule. It was a matter of gleaning real information on train departures from all the rumors that were floating around. Then it was important to be positioned to get onto that train fast, before it overfilled, while hoping that it would leave soon. Angela was sent back to the house to fetch more things, and that was the last we would ever see of her. Some time after our departure, though, Aunt Mimi had a chance to check on things at our old home, and Angela opened the door wearing clothes belonging to my mother. Mimi took a few things she thought we would like to have, including all the rolls of 8mm film that my father, an enthusiastic amateur photographer and filmmaker, had created, and a silver coffee percolator that had come down to my mother from hers. I would not see our house again until some thirty years later, as a tourist, and then only from the outside. By this time, I had lived in the United States for more than a decade. I had met my mother in Germany and together we traveled by train to visit family in what is today southwestern Poland. My cousins took turns being my guide to historical sites and places that had meaning for me from my childhood, including Hindenburg, my old home-town. When the items Mimi recovered were returned to us during our visit, it turned out that the coffeemaker was only silver plate, and the films were a box full of tangle. While most of the photos and films depicted our family, and a few were cartoons for the kids, there had also been some that my father had taken to record polit-ical speeches, events and meetings that included high-ranking Nazis and even Hitler. Aunt Mimi had discarded those because they would have been dangerous to possess if the Russian occupation troops had searched her home. Maybe the boys helped her seek those out, which must have been a challenge without a projector.

At the train station, we had been lucky enough to be on the correct platform when the news spread that a train was getting ready to leave. We were not able to get into a compartment but found standing room in the corridor. My little brother sat in his stroller. By now, the news of our train had spread throughout the station and a crowd was swarming toward us. A soldier standing next to us had the presence of mind to grab little Micky, pull him out of his fur cocoon and hold him up high above his head. This was good timing because the stroller got trampled by the desperate crowd fighting to get onto the train. Eventually, the train started moving. Little did we know that we were leaving behind not only our home and all our belongings, but an entire way of life.

I cannot remember how long the trip was. On both sides of the track, we saw the extent of the destruction: burned-out houses, ruined factories, and cratered landscapes. A couple of times, the train stopped. Sometimes, we could hear bombing nearby and if it was standing still, some of the people left the train to take cover on the tracks underneath. Other times, we could not discern the reason for the delay and simply had to wait and hope that we would soon be moving again. Finally, we arrived, tired but unhurt, and were greeted by Aunt Erna's parents. The old baker and his wife were living on the third floor of the building that housed the bakery and storefront shop at street level. His son, Aunt Erna's brother, Fred, lived on the second floor with his wife.

Already, Aunt Erna's sister with her toddler son had taken refuge with the old couple. Her husband had also been called up. Now with us arriving, there were five adults and three young children crammed into an apartment with two bedrooms. It was too dangerous to go out into the streets. Everybody was exhausted and stressed out. The children could find relief in crying and screaming. The adults had to remain civil with one another. The house had a flat roof, which I remember being covered with moss and the plant that I only know as hen and chicks. There we went for fresh air and the European ritual of sun-bathing. There were no guardrails, so it was impossible to leave a small child unattended for even a minute.

My mother, driven by hunger and stress, would soon start leaving us in the care of Aunt Erna and venture out early in the morning or at dusk. She found some abandoned garden plots on the edge of town where she gathered anything edible to supplement our diet of bread. She brought home green tomatoes, a few potatoes, and some string beans. One day she came back distraught. Many of the gardens had little shacks where the owners would keep lawn furniture, garden tools, supplies and enough utensils for casual meals. One of those looked especially inviting, and thinking to herself how sweet it would be to have even such a small space all to ourselves, she went inside. There she found a dead German soldier with flies buzzing all over his body. I do not know if she went out foraging again.

The highlight of the day for us children was evening, when my mother took Micky and me downstairs into the silent bakery. There among the big kettles for the mixing of the dough along with the tables and ovens for bread-making, she took us by the hands. We sang together, danced and ran and jumped around until we were lightheaded and tired and could be tucked in on the pallet that had been prepared for us upstairs.

Eventually, the Russian front advanced even closer. The conditions in which we lived were untenable for the long run. Returning home was not an option. So we fled farther west again. I cannot remember how we traveled, nor why the little town of Leitmeritz, where we knew no one, was selected as a destination. Chances are that it was because some sort of transportation was available. In a district of villas on the edge of town behind a little park, we found rooms in the house of an elderly widow, who was glad to have the company. Frau Korb had lived in Japan as a young woman with her missionary husband and had a houseful of fascinating pictures and souvenirs from there.

Hunger was now a serious issue. Bakeries and shops were open only if they had something to sell. It was a matter of luck and persistence to put anything on the table. We had several Mason jars of potted pork, with the pieces of meat settled on the bottom of the glass. The upper half consisted of congealed lard. But there was nothing to eat with this. So my mother took us children to some already harvested fields nearby, beyond a railroad track. There, we gleaned the ears of wheat that the harvesters, birds, and field mice had missed. At home, these were threshed on the kitchen table with a rolling pin. Then I got to help by grinding the grains in a big coffee grinder, which I held between my knees. Finally, my mother prepared a porridge for us all.

Days were peaceful; at least, I cannot remember many air raids there. The town was too small to be considered a worthy target. Once, there was a rumor of a bombing raid later that day that would flatten Leitmeritz to the ground with no stone left on top of another. Like almost everyone else, we left town and settled down at the edge of some woods. But nothing happened and as dusk came, it seemed more dangerous to remain out there in the open, surrounded by so many desperate strangers with unknown intentions, than to go back to Leitmeritz. Like many others, we took our chances and walked home.

I will now tell a story of which I am not sure I have any recollection beyond some visual memories. But I have heard it told so many times that I know it to be true.

During the last days of the war, a curious lull had settled over the little town. The only news was of a couple in a neighboring house, who had been found by a neighbor having hanged themselves in the attic. This was not uncommon. In mid-afternoon, two men came down the middle of our street pulling a handcart, stopping now and then and looking at the house numbers as though they were searching for a particular address. The little cart was loaded with food: sausages and loaves of bread, identifiable even from a distance. My Aunt Erna, never the shy one, went out and told them that if they were looking for a place to unload their cart, our house would be a good choice.

They came inside and a spread was put on the table the likes of which we had not seen in some time. Along with the food, there was also alcohol, particularly welcomed by Aunt Erna, who many years later was to die from the effects of alcoholism. As the party got into full swing, the men started to talk. Our town was situated only a short distance from the notorious concentration camp Theresienstadt (Teresien). It turned out that our two new friends had been working there, maybe as guards, but sensing that the war would be over in a matter of days, they deserted, taking with them what food they could gather.

As the drink relaxed their sense of caution, they started bragging about some of the things they had done. They told about a contest in which they had subjected their respective victims to what sounds like the torture now called waterboarding. My mother and Aunt Erna were appalled, not only on moral grounds but also because of the danger that the presence of these men in our house posed for us. After a few stressful hours, the two were finally persuaded, I do not know how, to leave with their handcart of food.

These were indeed the last days of the war. There was no longer any official news on the radio. Newspapers had long since ceased publication. Conversations with neighbors were the only source of any information. I remember endless discussions of the slim likelihood that, in the end, we might be occupied by British troops. The handwriting on the wall was writ large: we lay straight in the path of the advancing Russian army. The reputation of the Russian soldiers was fearsome, especially reports of their raping of women. My mother and Aunt Erna made a pact with each other: they would not be raped. After a few days, the news spread, I believe by word of mouth, that the war had ended. Germany had surrendered and Hitler was dead.

My mother and Aunt Erna had their stories ready. My mother, born to a Polish-German family in a part of the world that had been one or the other at different times in her life, had grown up speaking both languages with equal fluency. By now, she was so emaciated that she could hardly stand upright for long without leaning on something. Her story was that she was, in fact, a survivor of Theresienstadt, the nearby concentration camp. Looking at her, no one would have doubted that. If asked, she would say that Frau Korb, our landlady, had kept us children safe during my mother's confinement. That gave some sort of cover for two of the three women in the house. But my Aunt Erna, who was fully German, knew nothing more of any foreign language than a few scraps of French left over from her boarding school days. She decided to present herself as a deranged person. Unwashed, with dirty hair hanging into her face, she went around mumbling, carrying a large hammer in one hand and a fistful of nails in the other.

In our backyard, there was a big hole where earlier a wooden crate filled with food had been buried for safekeeping. Maybe that is where the Mason jars of pork and lard had come from. This hole the two young women decided to leave open. They were determined that any Russian soldier attempting to rape either one of them would get killed with the hammer and then be buried in that hole. Mercifully, it never came to that. For maybe as long as two weeks, soldiers singly or in small groups would come to our house, but not the hordes that were rumored to be roaming in mid-town. We were protected by the park between us and the center of town and so were missed by most of the roving gangs.

A few times survivors from the concentration camp also came to our house. But whether these people were looking for something other than three terrified women and two traumatized kids, or whether they were scared off by my Aunt Erna, no one ever tried to hurt us. One Russian soldier even gave us children each a small piece of chocolate, which came out of a round, flat tin and was dark and bitter. The worst scare we had more than two weeks after war's end was a late-night pounding on the door. We had no choice but to open it. A group of armed Russian soldiers, maybe six of them under the command of a sergeant or officer, came into the house and searched it from the cellar to the attic without any explanation. We assumed they were looking for hidden German soldiers. I remember sitting next to my mother on the side of a bed. She was holding Micky on her lap, and she held my hand and would encouragingly squeeze it. I have bad dreams about this experience even to this day. Had they found as much as a single uniform button, what might have happened to us is scary to imagine.

I think my Aunt Mimi, Uncle Emil, and cousins Felix and Jurek, together with their loyal maid Maria, had joined us by about that time. Uncle Emil, who had been drafted into the *Volkssturm*, a civilian fighting force similar to our National Guard, had deserted, and until the end of the war he could not safely remain where people knew him. How they were able to locate us, I cannot imagine. Beyond space in our crowded shelter, there was really nothing we could offer, neither food nor security. I imagine that they joined us mainly for the comfort of being with family. Mimi had stayed at home when the war ended and the Russian occupation began. She wanted to be where her son, Marian, now sixteen, could find her. When all hope was gone that he would show up, she had to assume that he had been made a prisoner of war. She gave up and left.

By now, the worst of the end-of-war upheaval was over. Some of the bakeries were beginning to operate again. I was happy to have my cousins there. Together, we explored the whole house of Frau Korb and, little by little, we spirited some of her many Japanese souvenirs and a large stamp collection out of the house and to a hiding place in the garden. When it finally became obvious that much of her Japanese collection was missing, we were interrogated, and in the end, we confessed tearfully. Our mothers made us give our stash back and apologize to Frau Korb.

It must have been during that time when one day in the middle of the afternoon, two Russian soldiers came to the house. They settled down at the kitchen table and asked for tea, which was prepared for them. One of them was a good-looking blond boy with blue eyes, whom everybody instantly liked; the other was scary-looking, swarthy, and slant-eyed. They would not let Maria, my aunt Mimi's pretty maid, out of their sight and eventually flanked her, sitting at the kitchen table and singing Russian songs to her from both sides. Toward evening, they started speaking to each other in rapid Russian and then the scary-looking boy left the house while the other one tried to persuade Maria to go with him. She declined, then, in panic, appealed to Aunt Mimi to explain to him that she was not allowed to leave the house at night.

In the end, the Russian grabbed Maria by the arm and, with Aunt Mimi trying to hang on to her, yanked her away and out of the house. We heard her crying out and the sound of scuffling outside. Within minutes, she rushed back into the house with blood gushing from a wound in her leg. She had been able to fend off the soldier, but an artery in her leg had been cut either by a boot or the butt of his rifle. I remember all the adults rushing around in panic and wrapping her leg tightly in towels to stem the stream of blood. I cannot remember whether a doctor could be found, but somehow the adults dealt with the situation successfully.

There was now no reason to stay in Leitmeritz, but no other good plan existed, either. Somehow, we got information about a man with a truck who might be available to transport us. The adults, in nightlong discussions, decided to hire him to take us all back to Jägerndorf, now Krnov, to the bakery of Aunt Erna's father. A collection of valuables was offered to pay the truck owner. Our meager possessions were loaded, and we all climbed into the bed of the truck, which I remember as a large one of the kind used then to transport goods on long distances. The back was covered with a tall rack and canvas tarp. The driver's girlfriend was in the cab with him, along for the ride. By nightfall, he stopped in a small town halfway to our destination and told us that the two of them would spend the night there in an inn. We spent our night in the bed of the truck, hidden under the tarp. Through the cracks, we could see Russian soldiers roaming the dark streets like cats on the prowl. In the morning, the man announced that he had decided to take us no farther—a ploy to extort more, maybe a couple more wristwatches, from us. In the end, he delivered us back to Jägerndorf, and the bakery.

Once again, we were all crowded into the top apartment above the bakery, but now with the addition of Aunt Mimi and her two boys. For some reason I don't think Uncle Emil was along. The bakery now had a new owner; a Czech with his family had taken it over. The former owner, Aunt Erna's father, was now the foreman. He was the only one who knew how to bake bread. Her brother and his wife were gone. (No worries, you will hear from him again.) My Aunt Mimi and her entourage, two boys and a maid, did not stay long but soon moved closer to their old home. During the few days when we were all together, an episode happened that has always seemed funny in retrospect: three Russian soldiers bivouacked in our apartment overnight. They hung out in the kitchen and occupied one of the bedrooms. We were all crowded into the other, afraid to step out.

By evening everybody was hungry and thirsty. Finally, my Aunt Mimi volunteered to go into the kitchen and make us some tea. There, she was approached by one of the soldiers, who tried to entice her with compliments on her looks. She maintained that she was an ugly old woman. He countered that she was not too old for love. The conversation took place in a mixture of Russian and

Polish. This went back and forth until Aunt Mimi took out her partial plate and smiled at him with a big gap in her teeth. He was still not to be discouraged. So, she took his hand with hers and placed it on the part of her belly where she wore a brace for a hernia. Due to the chaotic times and circumstances, the hernia had not been repaired. Who knows what the man thought when he was touching the hard contraption of leather and metal? He withdrew his hand as though stung by a wasp and bothered her no more.

A few other memories stick in my head from the weeks or months we lived there. The bakery faced onto a small square. One afternoon, a convoy of Russian trucks full of soldiers pulled up and parked in this square. Across the square was a house with a former flower shop that had been largely destroyed by a bomb. The owner, a woman in her eighties, continued to live in a couple of rooms still more or less intact. As we would learn later, she decided, since she could not lock the ruined door anyway, that her best course of action was to act friendly toward the Russians. It was late at night when we heard her screaming, "*Hilfe!* Help! Help!" It was hard not going to her aid. We had to restrain Aunt Erna from going downstairs. Eventually, the screaming stopped. The next day, the woman proudly told everybody that two Russian soldiers had violently fought over her, and she showed us the blood stains on the wall to prove it. An officer, wakened by her screaming, had finally broken up the fight. The two adversaries had been handcuffed and taken into custody, one of them with a big, bloody bandage wrapped around his head. Their convoy left during the day.

Another night we woke up from the sound of shouting, talking, and crying in the street below. Without turning on the lights, we peeked through cracks in the curtains. Armed soldiers were roughly marching a crowd of civilians, including children, past the house. The throng passed below our window for a long time. There had to be hundreds of them, and whence they had come or where they were driven remains a painful mystery to me. At other occasions torch parades went through the streets, celebrating we did not know what.

For a while, my Aunt Erna lived with us illegally. I think my mother must have registered us with the new authorities as Polish, but it was deemed too dangerous for Aunt Erna to register as a German. She would immediately have been placed in a camp and been separated from us. I remember that for some time, she hid out in the cemetery during daylight hours, and we went there to take her a little food and drink. I cannot remember how long this went on. What I can remember is that Aunt Erna was a smoker and was desperate for anything resembling a cigarette. The new Czech bakery owners and the neighboring businesses got to know my mother and would offer her cigarettes. She was not a smoker then and cigarettes made her cough, but Aunt Erna implored her not to refuse the offers but to light up, take a puff or two, then stub the cigarette out and bring the rest of it home. This was how my mother, at first reluctantly, became a smoker of cigarettes, a habit that she could not entirely shed for the remainder of her life.

The new Czech bakery owner and his wife had two sons about my age. I think they also had a younger girl. I started playing with the boys and quickly picked up a few Czech words. This gave my mother the idea of enrolling me in the Czech school. A German language school was not available, and it had been a long time since I had seen the inside of a classroom. I was not the only German child in my class. In the beginning, I was barely able to follow what was going on. But soon I could take part in the classwork, with my brain filling in, sometimes fancifully and not always accurately, the gaps in my understanding. To this day, I can recite the opening words of the Czech national anthem and sing parts of several little songs, which we learned in school or from the radio.

Not so different from my experience in first grade in Germany, indoctrination of young minds was practiced here, too. We were taught to sing the national anthem, *"Gde domov moj?"* ("Where Is

My Home?"). And we learned much about the life and virtues of the country's president. On festival days, the girls would come to school in spectacular ethnic dress: a fitted sleeveless top over a white blouse with large, lace-trimmed sleeves, a full skirt and a half apron. They would wear wreaths of flowers in their hair. I wished fervently to own such an outfit, a wish I made come true in 1972 when, after more than ten years in the US, I made my first visit back to the land of my early childhood. I bought the Polish version of such a dress in the re-built center of Warsaw, where my cousins were my guides. By a lucky accident when later we were on a train returning to my aunt's, a fellow passenger in our compartment, with whom we struck up a conversation, told us that he had been one of the team of architects who had rebuilt and restored the bombed-out center of Warsaw.

I have one bad memory from my Czech school experience. During physical education, when we were practicing Czech folk dancing in preparation for some holiday presentation, I made some wrong move, and the woman teacher came up to me and gave me a hard slap in the face. I am pretty sure that she did this not because I had been a klutz but because I was a German child. Who knows what she had experienced to have such strong resentments.

Just a few days ago, a friend and I were in Boerne in the Texas Hill Country on a day trip, and we happened to find Little Gretel, a Czech restaurant. It looked so inviting that we decided to eat our dinner there. The help was friendly, and for no good reason I told the server that seventy-five years ago I had attended a Czech school. Soon the Czech chef came to our table to chat. She and I sang a duet of a children's song which I still know by heart. This scene is now featured in a video on the restaurant's Facebook site.

Beyond a slap in the face and one song about Anitchka in her cabbage patch and fragments of other songs, there is one memory that I am still processing more than seventy-five years later. I already mentioned that I played with the two boys of the Czech family, who were about my age. When I say "played" I really do not remember more than walking to school together, eating snacks from the bakery, and learning enough of the other's language to communicate. One day one of the boys asked me if I would like to play and he said a word I did not know. I said "Yes" and forgot about it. Some days later he asked me again and I asked him "How does the game go?" He answered, "you and I both take our underpants off, and I stick my *churak* into your behind." I had never heard that word, but I instantly knew what it meant. The entire sentence is burned into my memory. I told him "I don't want to play that game," and that was the end of it. I did not tell my mother or anybody else. But I have often thought how little we parents sometimes know of what goes on in the heads and the lives of our children.

I have, together with their fathers, raised four children, two of my own and two step- or as I prefer "bonus" children from my second marriage. When I hear them reminiscing, I learn things that happened or thoughts they had thought, of which I knew nothing, and I must ask them, "Now tell me, what house did you grow up in?" The important thing is that today I am on good terms with all four of them.

But back to my story: My mother was unhappy because of the crowded quarters and her lack of control over any aspect of our lives. She and Aunt Erna were considering alternatives. We got together with old acquaintances and made some new friends, exchanging information in hopes of finding a solution. My Aunt Erna was worried about her younger brother, Kurt, who had been drafted and of whom the family had not had any news in a long time. There were women who claimed to possess psychic powers that enabled them to divine whether a particular person was alive or dead. There was plenty of business for them, as practically every family had somebody whose whereabouts were unknown. The divination was done with a golden wedding ring suspended by a thread and dangled over a photograph of the missing person. Depending on the direction the ring began to swing, the practitioners of this magic then announced the answer, usually a positive one. I imagine those women were being paid for their service with food, the currency of the time. Did they believe in their own powers? Despite encouraging pronouncements after several of these sessions, Aunt Erna's family never learned Kurt 's fate. He must have fallen in action or have died in a prisoner-of-war camp.

During this time my mother and I also made a couple of trips to visit Aunt Mimi and her family in their new quarters. This meant going illegally across the border between what was now Czechoslovakia, where we lived, and what had become western Poland, where they lived. We went by train to a stop close to the border and then walked through fields and past the kilns of an abandoned brick factory, crossing the border at some point. In a small village on the Polish side, a man waited for us with a horse and cart. I remember that I was not afraid when we were sneaking across the border. To an eight-year-old, it seemed like an adult version of hide-and-seek. But I, a city child until then, was terrified of the buggy ride and imagined a variety of ways in which we might crash and all die in a ditch.

In long palavers during these visits, the decision hardened in my mother's mind that we should somehow get to the western zone of Germany, which was occupied by the American military. Aunt Mimi and her family, in the end, decided to stay where they were, mainly for two reasons: my Oma, then probably in her late sixties, did not want to leave her parents' graves and the grave of my Opa. Both she and Mimi still hoped for the safe return of their sons, Hansi and Marian, respectively. They wanted to be where the men, upon their return, would be able to find them. In the end, both men survived the war but had endured years of internment in Russian prison camps, where they suffered irreparable damage to their physical and psychic health. For the time being, my two younger cousins, Felix and Jurek, were getting into plenty of mischief without the help of their uncle and older brother.

There was no electricity in Aunt Mimi's village at that time. The only source of light was *carbitkas*, tin lamps with a wick, maybe something the miners might have used, which produced a lot of smelly fumes and only dim illumination. They were fueled with chunks of yellowish-white stuff called carbide, hence their name. While the adults were weighing the pros and cons of the poor options available, we kids roamed the streets. One source of trouble was that weapons and ammunition could be easily found in ditches or middens, along with German uniforms, where they had been tossed by German soldiers. The boys gathered the cartridges and quickly figured out how to remove the lead bullets to get to the black powder, with which they could make lovely little fireworks. It was tough to pry the lead tip off the cartridges. I guess that was what prompted them to put one into a lighted burner on the kitchen range. We all got a big fright when the shell exploded. The parents made sure there was no more playing of that game.

My mother, even though she also knew nothing about the fate of my father, her husband, was unwilling to remain. No one knew at the time that this choice would become irreversible. The artificial friendship between the Russians and their Western allies soon crumbled, leading to the so-called Cold War. The Berlin Wall went up, the Iron Curtain came down, and all my Polish relatives became stuck behind it, separating us from the rest of our family. It would be decades before the family could gather in person again.

While we had already lost most of our possessions, along with the home we had abandoned, we still had some items of value: personal jewelry, gold coins, bank records, and such. All Germans were under strict orders to surrender such property to the Czech government. My mother and Aunt Erna were acquainted with a certain Mr. Jablonski. I think he had been a friend, maybe lover, of Aunt Mimi's. How we communicated with him I cannot imagine.

He, with a Polish passport, could cross the border between Poland-Czechoslovakia and "the West" with only modest bureaucratic hurdles. He agreed to take valuable items that my Aunt Erna had left at her parents' and told us how we could find him once we were in West Germany. One item I remember because I found it so interesting and spent many hours with it was a large book, a special edition, bound in white calfskin, which contained images and descriptions of the entire body of work of Leonardo da Vinci. We never were able to find Mr. Jablonski again, but Aunt Erna was philosophical. She would have lost this treasure anyway.

3. Deportation and Resettlement

Having decided to leave for the West, my mother and Aunt Erna made a plan, which was precariously executed by registering us all as Germans with the authorities. This meant that we were forced to move into a camp, formerly for prisoners of war. There, we lived with strangers, in barracks that were furnished only with rough bunk beds. The straw sacks for mattresses were crawling with bedbugs, which remained nearly invisible during daylight but covered us with painful bites as soon as the lights went out. There was no insecticide, no fumigation material, no possible change of mattress, no way even to reduce the number of these awful bloodsuckers. People had to get creative. During daytime, the adults took the straw sacks off the bunks and looked them over carefully, especially the seams where the bedbugs liked to hide. They speared the bugs with long darning needles and then incinerated each victim in a candle flame, with a little crackling noise and the smell of burned hair. This was a daily chore. The bugs probably reproduced faster than they could be killed. Our daily food was horrible slop from the camp kitchen. The latrines were communal, foul-smelling cesspools. Many people got sick and died, especially infants. I knew the German word for "rape" as something shameful, even though I did not understand the reason. I also knew the word "infected," as apparently syphilis was rampant among the Russians.

We learned many years later that my other Aunt Erna, my father's sister by the same name, had been in a labor camp for German women and had been repeatedly raped. After a day of forced labor, when the exhausted young women were in their barracks, Russian soldiers would go through the wards with flashlights. They would shine into the faces of the women and girls and pull some out of their beds by force. A few of the women tried to cultivate a friendship with one particular guard to be protected from these nightly atrocities. This "other" Aunt Erna was later reunited with her husband in the Russian-occupied zone of Germany when he returned from a prison camp, and together they built a new existence for themselves with an ice cream parlor, where they thrived because their ice cream, made with West German ingredients supplied by my father, was much more delicious than that of their competitors. Unfortunately, they were denounced, and when it was discovered that much of that ice cream had been sold under the table, so to speak, they were both thrown into East German jails and their house was confiscated by the state. Somehow, after their release from prison, she and her husband were able to relocate to West Germany, where she later, a widow by then, re-entered my mother's and distantly my life. She had become a bitter and confused old woman, suspicious and hard to get along with. No wonder, considering the horrors she had experienced.

In our camp, there was the daily *Apell* (assembly) when, at the sound of a siren, all had to line up outside their barracks and stand at attention, sometimes for hours. Guards came and put together work parties. Luckily, my mother never got picked for one of those, but Aunt Erna was pressed into service and had to perform road work with a pick and shovel under armed guard. She lifted everybody's spirits when she led the brigade out of the camp, singing, with their tools shouldered. There was no singing when they trudged back into camp in the late afternoon, exhausted.

Now and then, giving us hope, a transport of camp inhabitants was assembled and sent in freight trains across the Western border. This was years before the Iron Curtain came down and trapped those who had not left while leaving was still possible. During our time in the camp, which lasted only a few months, we discovered a hole under the barbed wire fence. My mother and Aunt Erna would send me into town through that hole with letters hidden in my shoe, addressed to the parents of Aunt Erna or some of our friends. I felt proud and important when they called me their little carrier pigeon. In the afternoon, carrying fresh bread and other foods, I simply walked back into the camp through the main gate, along with other people, and was never questioned.

Eventually, our numbers came up. We got little slips of paper and were told to get ready to be transported to the West the next day. Everyone was warned that it was forbidden to take any valuable personal property with them, and we were exhorted to hand over any remaining valuables at this last chance. Both my and Micky's warm winter coats had the last of our horde of gold coins sewn into the hems. Also, my mother still had some jewelry left and she still had the ending pages from our bank records. During that last night in our barracks, my mother and Aunt Erna were busy hiding these things in Micky's stroller: the bank records, rolled up tightly, were slipped into the push-bar, the jewelry "glued" with candle wax under the padding of his back rest.

My little brother had been fussy for a couple of days and by now was running a fever, but my mother concealed this fact from the guards. Her greatest fear was that we would be separated. The next day, we were loaded into freight cars, thirty persons and their meager belongings to each car. My mother had some aspirin and this she gave to Micky with a little water flavored with raspberry syrup. She used an enameled cup to warm it over a candle. The trip, as best I can remember, took two or three days. Now and then the train stopped, and people rushed from the train and into the fields and bushes to relieve themselves. At these stops, some "camp soup" was brought around. The landscapes which we saw through the open door of the rail car were getting lovelier as we traveled west. Gone were the drab and bombed cities. Now we were passing through undulating meadows and woods, dotted with villages clustered around onion-domed churches, the houses neat with flower boxes on the windowsills and in the little gardens. Cows were placidly grazing, the bells around their necks clanking as they moved about.

Eventually, we arrived in Augsburg, Bavaria, in the American-occupied part of Germany. The first triage occurred in the great hall of a castle, which had been organized as a processing camp. There, we were herded through some makeshift showers and then had to line up, men, women, and children, all naked as the day we were born, for a cursory physical exam, a couple of immunizations, and a puff of DDT, administered by a large hand-pumped spray gun directed under each arm and to the crotch. Micky, who was burning with fever by now, was immediately taken to a hospital; the diagnosis was measles. The rest of us, like all the family units, were allotted a blanket. These were spread on the floor of the great hall as each family's temporary quarters. Some food was distributed. We stayed in this camp only for a day or two and then were transported to another, smaller camp in Marktoberdorf, the gym of a school building with similar accommodations.

From there, after a matter of days, several other families and we were loaded onto a flatbed trailer pulled by a tractor, a rig that on regular days would have been used for bringing in the hay. The tractor went from small village to small village. The last of these was Enisried, where we would live for the next five years. At that time, there was a huge influx of displaced persons from the Eastern provinces of Germany into the Western ones, but no extra housing stock was available. Not only had there been no residential construction for most of the six war years, but much of the cities' housing had been destroyed by bombs, although not nearly to the same extent as in the more industrialized north and east. The Allied Occupation Forces, as a provisional government, had decreed that every local family had to make room in their house for one family unit of refugees. One-by-one, the other families on the flatbed found places to stay.

My mother, Aunt Erna, and I—two skinny young women and a small girl (Micky was still in the hospital at Augsburg)—were the last ones left on that trailer. The driver, who apparently knew which of the houses had not yet found their refugee match, took us to the farm of a man and his two sisters, all unmarried. They resisted the idea of taking us in. All three of them were outside the front door, not just symbolically barring our entrance. One of the sisters was sweeping the front walk in great agitation. Their reason for refusing us, quite freely articulated, was that we did not look like we could be of any help with the work on the farm, which they felt was unfair to them. By now, it was late afternoon. We had had no food or drink since the camp breakfast. Today I view this painful experience somewhat differently. Here, in Texas, where I am quite comfortably residing, comes another influx of distressed people from many parts of the world who are seeking a safe place. If the authorities now asked me "Ms. Grieder, which part of your home would you like to make available to these immigrants?" would I be as welcoming as we expected these people to be? The best I could answer would be "That depends." I have taken into my house for limited times friends and even a couple of women whom I did not know, women who needed a safe place to stay but did not have the means to rent space. Immigrants of unknown qualities and characters would be a different matter.

It started to sprinkle, and the man driving the tractor wanted to head for home. Only after he threatened to call in the local refugee ombudsman did the three residents relent. Reluctantly, they led us to a spare bedroom upstairs, which they had been using for storage. My Aunt Erna prevailed on them to remove from the room several bicycles and a few pairs of old shoes. Several sacks of grain stacked in a corner of the room, in which we could often hear the mice rustling around, stayed there for the entire few weeks of our stay in this house. In the morning after our first night, there was a knock on our door. One of the sisters brought a small pitcher of fresh milk that had a thick slice of bread as a lid. It must have been Sunday because she asked if we wanted to go to church. We politely declined. No sooner had the three taken off for church, three miles away, on their bicycles, than my Aunt Erna found and raided the hen house. We had a nice breakfast of eggs with that slice of bread. I was instructed not to tell anyone about this, but it was also explained to me that we were entitled to these eggs on two grounds: 1) the people of the house had lost the war the same as we had without suffering the slightest harm, and 2) devout Catholics that they were, they should have given us those eggs and more in the first place.

It must have been at least a day or two before I even ventured out through the front door for the first time. When I finally did, there were several children about my age standing in a row facing the door. It was big news in this hamlet of thirteen houses that there was a new kid. No telling how long they had been waiting there to get a glimpse of me. I cannot remember how many children there were or who was there on that first day. All I can still see, when I close my eyes, is that one of them was eating a large slice of homemade bread, thickly spread with butter and jam. My eyes still fill with tears when I see that mental picture and remember how hungry I was. I think this is why I always have too much food in the house.

My mother missed my little brother, who was still in the

hospital in Augsburg, a long train trip away, recovering from the measles. There was no way to communicate with him. She spoke about him all the time, and everybody was curiously awaiting the little wonder child. When the day to bring him home finally arrived, she could hardly wait for our landlords to return from their fields so she could show him off. The nuns who worked at the hospital, whom little Micky was told to address as "Dear Auntie," had cut Micky's long hair. Likely, it was a precautionary procedure for all their young patients, since almost everyone coming from the camps in the East zone was covered with lice. They used the bowl-method for their barbering. When our three hosts saw the little guy, they broke out in loud laughter and, pointing their fingers at him, they cried out, "Look, look, a Russ! A Russ!" This, more than their meanness and stinginess, poisoned the well of our relationship with them forever.

My first circle of friends was in the hamlet: my two classmates Joseph (Seppl) Kugler and Klara and a few other children about our age. Our first ball was one which my mother sewed for us from lozenge-shaped scraps of fabric and stuffed with straw. It did not bounce and was not much fun to play with. Later someone would become the owner of a volleyball, or a soccer ball, but in the beginning, we had to invent other games. One of our favorites was "building a house," a variant of hide-and-seek. The person who was "it" used three pieces of split wood to erect a kind of pyramid, the "house." Everybody else hid. The person who was "it" had to close their eyes and count to a certain number, say thirty, while we found our hiding places. I think the inside of the house was off limits. When the person who was "it" detected one of those who were hiding, they had to run to the "house," put their foot inside and call out the name of the found person, who was now a prisoner and had to stay on the sidelines. If the person who was "it" roamed too far from "house," one of the hidden kids could come and topple the pyramid and any prisoners were freed. That was always done with gusto by running up and kicking the structure so that the three pieces of split wood flew in three directions. Whoever had the bad luck to be "it" was stuck in that role for the rest of the day. Later, when we had some real balls, we played *Volkerball,* which required a minimum of six players, not always available.

A couple of fathers each rigged a long rope onto the top of the tall door opening to their hayloft. We kids scrounged a little board, maybe eight by eighteen inches, just large enough for two kids placing their feet side by side on it. We notched it at the two short sides, so it would stay in place, and put it into the looped rope. Voila, a great swing! We would double up, face to face, and start swinging. Since the loft doors were tall, the swing had a large arc, and we were always pushing the envelope, swinging higher and higher so that it was not uncommon for a passerby to cross him- or herself. A few times the little piece of wood split and fell off and our poor naked feet, with our full weight, were on the rope. We all wore shoes to school, but during the summer they came off as soon as we got home. In the spring my feet were very tender, but soon they got tough. It was expected that sooner or later we would step on a bee and get stung. When it rained, as it often does close to the Alps, we played cards or read or squabbled.

I was soon enrolled in school in the larger village of Seeg, where the church was located, about three miles from our hamlet, Enisried. According to my age, I was put into third grade even though I had only attended a portion of first grade and no second grade except for the couple of months in Czech school. Klara and Joseph, of our hamlet, were also in third grade, and we decided to make the long walk to school together every morning.

There are many distractions on a three-mile walk for three eight-year-olds, which meant that we arrived late for class almost every day. Sometimes we were so late that we could not agree on a plausible excuse, and rather than facing the music, we would turn around and go home again. To explain why we had missed school, we would all agree that we would tell our parents that we met a child, whom we had never seen before and whose name we did not know, who was coming back from Seeg, and who had told us that the teacher was ill and that classes had been canceled, or some story along such lines. The next day we would tell the teacher the same story. I find it hard to believe that our tales convinced any of the adults, but we all stuck to the same account and there was little they could do.

When the long days of summer started to get shorter, we hated to see the season end. In late fall crocus-like, lavender-colored little flowers popped up all over the meadows. In German called *Herbstzeitlose* (autumn-timeless), the flower is a harbinger of the short dark days of winter. Lovely though it is, we hated to see it and stomped each flower along our path. Later, when the first freeze-nights left a thin crust of ice on all the puddles, we did the same, stomping on them to break the ice. Another distraction was a small chapel, called *Pestfriedhof* (Plague Cemetery), to which a sign at the road directs the traveler. It was about a quarter mile from the country road, surrounded by a group of conifers in a large meadow. A historical marker told that here was the mass-grave of the victims of the last plague that had ravaged Europe, in the sixteenth century. It was a somber little place, a tiny chapel with its onion dome. The altar piece is a painting that I do not remember well and would love to see once more in my life. It seems to me that it depicted a saint holding a skull. As usual in these paintings, I think it, too, included in a smaller scale, in the lower right corner of the picture, the donors in their black medieval Sunday best. Recently when the Covid virus made its appearance all over the world, I often thought of this little chapel, and how much we were in the same place more than five hundred years later. We, like the people who are resting there, were stricken by a deadly plague. Like them, we did not know how it was transferred and how to protect ourselves. I have heard that the men who gathered the dead and transported them to places like this mass grave believed that drinking alcohol protected them against contagion. The first symptoms were probably similar to those of Covid, or a cold, or flu: sore throat, coughing, and sneezing. I believe this is why we say "Gesundheit," "Salud," or "Yasha" (Turkish for "live") to one who sneezes, and "To your good health," "*À votre santé,*" when we clink glasses.

Winter came early in southern Bavaria. The only fuels available at that time were split logs and to a lesser degree peat. In late fall, all the houses had large wood stacks. Peat was dug during the summer in a marshy area close to the woods. I don't know whether this was communally owned land, or whether one had to pay the owner to dig there. The top layer was paler in color, fibrous, not very heavy, and might have served well for starting a fire. The good stuff lay deeper, was much darker, smoother, and very heavy. The peat was carved in brick-shaped pieces in layers just the way stone is cut from a quarry. The tool was a long-handled blade, with which the cutter cut the outline of the brick, and then cut it underneath and lifted it. When ground water appeared, the cutter stopped going deeper. The bricks were stacked two on two crosswise in waist-high columns and left to dry.

Sometime before the first snow, usually in November, Father Geller and Seppl would plant stakes on both sides of the dirt path that led from our house to the hamlet, with little bunches of spruce boughs tied to the top, similar to the gates for slalom skiing. One could then tell where the path ran even after a big snowfall. Our cold, three-mile walk to school started in pitch dark. If it had snowed during the night, we children would be the first ones to make footprints, and the fresh snow wanted to stick heavily to our shoes. Sometimes we got lucky, and someone had walked ahead of us, usually an adult. Then we would take long strides trying to take advantage of the existing footprints. When we arrived, we always had clumps of ice clinging to the tops of our shoes and to the bottom of our pants, which would slowly melt in the warm class-room and make puddles under our feet.

I think it was my mother's boyfriend, the cheese maker, who rounded up some old, rusty ski bindings somewhere in an attic and had the village carpenter make a pair of skis for me. Alas, lumber was valuable. The skis turned out a bit too short for me and got even shorter as I kept growing. This, combined with my fear of getting hurt, kept me from ever getting beyond a quite modest skiing ability, while the local children fearlessly raced down the steepest inclines. Still, it made getting to school easier than walking. In the summer, the local children rode bicycles. It was a couple of years before we owned one, which we shared among the three of us.

I remember quite well our third-grade teacher, Herr Pfitzner. He was a kind man; not all of them were kind. All our regular teachers were men. Many had suffered from the war and its after-math, had lost limbs or been wounded otherwise, or their nerves had been wrecked. This teacher was progressive for the times. It was the custom then for German children to sit in class any time they were not actually working, with their hands together on their desks, straight in front of them, four fingers on the desktop, thumbs beneath. On day one, Herr Pfitzner said we would not have to sit that way anymore, that it constrained the chest and kept the lungs from expanding and doing their job properly. In the future, when listening to the teacher, we would put our hands on the desktop but keep them about a foot apart.

Physical punishment was still very much the rule in German schools in those days, but I never saw a girl being spanked. Boys, though, who had misbehaved badly, were occasionally struck with a rod on the palm of their held-out hand or spanked on their bottoms. Most of the local boys wore *Lederhosen*, short Bavarian-style pants made of leather and typically handed down and stiff from genera-tions of wear, and they were loose-fitting. In the interest of fairness, teachers would hit these boys harder because of the protection afforded them by those pants. Refugee boys, whose *Lederhosen* were more likely to be *ersatz*, made from cloth in the style of Bavarian leather pants, always urgently explained this important difference to the teacher before the first whack was administered.

Penmanship in cursive, for everyone, and needlework for the girls, were taught by a nun. Paper was still scarce. The slate I used had turned up in someone's attic and was on loan to me. I think it must have been very old. All along the lines, deep grooves had been worked into the surface by generations of school kids pressing down firmly with a hard stylus, and I could still make out the spiky shapes of some of the old-style, Gothic letters. In needlework, we learned to knit and crochet. There, our material was the yarn that had come from the unraveling of some worn-out piece of clothing, so it was very kinky-curly. I was lucky to be right-handed but pity the poor kid that would grasp either the pencil or the crochet hook with the left hand. The little miscreant promptly received a sharp rap on the offending hand, either with a large ruler or an oversized wooden demonstration crochet hook, depending on the lesson.

At home, the relationship with our three sibling landlords never could recover from its difficult start. If we helped ourselves to some eggs, they soon paid back in kind and ate some of the little food we had. I remember my mother once being able to get salted herrings on our meat rations when meat was not available, and she went to a lot of trouble to marinate those in the Swedish manner. There was not a single refrigerator in the entire village. But all the houses had cellars where the temperature stayed cool year-round. My mother asked permission to keep our herrings in the cellar during the curing process, but when she went downstairs to fetch them, she found that half of them had disappeared. One of the sisters explained that her brother Ludwig loved them so much, he had not been able to resist temptation. They offered no substitute for the missing herrings.

Through Seppl, I became acquainted with his parents and his house. Actually, it was little Micky who made friends with the farmer's wife, Frau Kugler. Long recovered from the measles, he now tagged behind me more often than I would have liked. It was he, at three and a half, who brought about a solution to our terrible living situation. He would walk into the kitchen of Seppl's parents, dressed in his darling city clothes, and immediately start to compliment the farm wife. "My, it smells so good in your kitchen. You must be making something very delicious," and so on, melting her good heart instantly. He not only got a treat stuffed into his little mouth but was sent home with something more in his pockets. The Kugler family had not yet taken in any refugees, and it was certain that they would have to do so, sooner or later. It occurred to them to offer us a room in their house, and we happily accepted. My classmate, Seppl, had two sisters, Annie, sixteen or seventeen, and Siegi, about twelve. So, there would be five kids in the house.

Not only were we welcome in our new quarters, but it was also a much better situation. The room was on the ground floor in the back of the house and must have been intended for a live-in grandmother or mother-in-law. It had windows on two walls, with green wooden shutters that were closed at night. It had its own little one-burner, cast-iron stove and was close to the back door, seldom used by the family, giving us a lot of privacy. We even had our own outhouse, connected to the stable that housed the cows. We had to step outside through the back door to enter it. That was no hardship during the short summer, but during the long, snowy winter months, it was a tough place to visit late at night or first thing in the morning.

My mother soon made our room into a cozy, *gemütlich,* little place, with some nice little pieces of original art on the wall and colorful cushions on the seating, which would be turned into beds at night. A fresh bouquet of wildflowers was always on the table. I loved arranging the flowers, which were abundant in the meadows right outside our door. She cooked our meals, such as they were, on that little stove, called a cannon-stove for its appearance and which had to be fed wood or pinecones from the top. She figured out that she could start one pot—say, the potatoes—and then start a second pot with whatever we would eat with the potatoes. She would then place the first pot on top of the second like a lid, where it would finish cooking from the steam beneath it. If she had something to bake, she was allowed to do so in the farm kitchen where the built-in kitchen range and oven had a good wood fire going most of the time.

Going in and out of the family's rooms and kitchen, I saw what they ate. Even though they had plenty of the things they produced like milk, butter, eggs, and vegetables from a kitchen garden, their food was not more interesting than ours. They ate all their meals in the *Herrgottswinkel* (Lord God's corner), a corner bench in the living room with a large eating table. On the wall above, in the corner, hung a crucifix with framed color lithographs of the Virgin Mary and St. John flanking it. For breakfast, they ate eggs and bread. Mid-morning, they took a break from fieldwork and ate homemade bread broken into cool milk, which they spooned from a communal bowl. Everyone had their assigned seat and where the farmer sat, there was a leather loop on the edge of the tabletop where he left his carefully licked spoon for the next meal. All the other flatware went to the kitchen to be washed. Lunch was the main meal but typically did not include meat except on Sundays. The evening meal was bread, butter and cheese, salami or ham, sometimes accompanied by a sharp radish, which had been spiral cut and salted. When ham or sausage was not available, they ate a hot porridge called *Brennsuppe* (burned soup), made from a roux of butter and flour. It was cooked to a dark brown color, to which water and cool milk were added at the table. I hated the scorched smell of the roux and never liked the taste of the finished product, no matter how hungry I was.

Even our host family knew that their food was plain. If my mother had to go to buy groceries in Seeg, three miles away, the daughters, Annie and Siegi, immediately suggested that we cook some mushroom and egg together: I would, from my mother's supplies, contribute dried mushrooms, which we soaked to rehydrate, and powdered egg, which was all we could get with our ration cards. They would supply the lard in which to fry these ingredients into patties. If my mother ever noticed that something was missing, she did not say.

Once a week, on Saturdays, my mother would stoke our little cannon stove and make the room very warm, especially during the winter. Then she brought her galvanized washtub in, set it on the floor close to the stove, and put on a large pot of water to heat. Micky was the first to get into the tub. While she gave him his bath, another pot of water would be heating to be added to the tub for me. Mother was the last one to take her bath.

She used the same tub for washing our laundry. There was no washing machine in the house. I doubt that such a luxury even existed anywhere in Germany at that time. My mother had a washboard, and, in the absence of washing powder, she used a large piece of a very basic soap. In the area between our room and the back door and the entrance to the main part of the house, there was a built-in vat above a little chamber in which a wood-fueled fire was built for boiling the white stuff. To dry, the laundry was hung on a line out in the open, and white items, especially if there might be a soap-resisting stain, were spread on the grass to bleach naturally from sunlight. When laundry was drying outdoors, we had to keep an eye out and chase away any chickens that might walk on it or the calves that more than once took a big bite out of somebody's cotton shirt. Even the basic rough soap could be hard to come by. I remember that our landlady once made her own, a smelly affair. She was doing this outside in a big kettle that she kept stirring with a paddle. The main ingredients were water, cracked cow bones and lye. There also was a well, close to the front door, but it was seldom used because to get at it, a round cover of stone or concrete had to be lifted and then one had to fill a bucket or other container. The water was clear, cool and delicious. There were little creatures living at the bottom of the well, not more than one or two at a time and two or three inches long. They were soft-bodied, and they collected tiny pebbles around their delicate skins like armor. I cannot recall the name for them. We left the little critters in peace, and they did nothing to spoil the water for us. I never knew what they ate.

One time after doing some washing, my mother glanced at her hands and, to her great dismay, noticed that her ring was missing its stone and she was looking at an empty setting. This was the engagement ring that my father had given her, and the missing stone was a respectable diamond. She was sad and upset. Without much hope she looked all over the area where she had been working and all around our room, but the diamond could not be found. Well, we had experienced much greater losses than this and she eventually, resignedly, stopped the search. Weeks later, after using the tub again, maybe for the Saturday bath routine, she was wiping it off when she was done, and with the tips of her fingers she felt something in the seam where the tub's wall was welded to its bottom. To her surprise and great joy, she had found the missing stone.

The side of that old house that was occupied by humans had two stories. On the ground floor were the living room, kitchen, corridor, the laundry area with the built-in copper kettle, a stairwell for access to the cellar, and our room. Upstairs, there were three bedrooms: the parents', Seppl's, and the one the two daughters shared. For all to share there was a bathroom containing a tub and an outhouse-type toilet, and finally a tiny room with a slant ceiling, carved out from the attic, where the hired hand would sleep, if there were one. The cow stable, with a huge hay barn above, was attached to the dwelling like the leg of an L. There was a connecting door from the corridor to the stable, and the whole house was suffused with the warm, rich smell of animals, hay, milk, and manure.

While we had no running water within our room, there was a water faucet right outside the hall for use in the laundry. At first, all four of us lived in that room, but soon Aunt Erna leased a small movie theater in Füssen, twenty-five or thirty miles due south, and we now saw her only occasionally. Her visits always turned into parties because Aunt Erna loved to drink. When she did, she became even more gregarious and funny than she was while sober. Everybody, refugee or local, was welcome to join the party. This soon gave rise to a little entrepreneurship. In this small hamlet, where there had never been anything stronger than milk for sale, one of the local families with whom we were quite friendly soon started stocking a few cases of beer so that Aunt Erna, on her visits, could buy rounds for everybody.

Even though we lived in a village of dairy farmers, food was our greatest concern from the first day of our arrival. Though there was plenty of it, it did not belong to us. The old Third Reich money was still around, but it was worthless. More than once I saw someone roll up a bill and light the rare pleasure of a cigarette with it from the fire in the stove. Matches were valuable and scarce. We had already eaten up two or three of the gold coins that had been stitched into the hem of my and Micky's winter coats and I think we had lost at least one when the stitches came loose. This could clearly not go on for long, so my mother started to help in the fields.

Living on a dairy farm, I learned first-hand what it means to make hay when the sun shines. It was some time after the end of the war that the various farmers were able to buy tractors. Until then everything was done with manual labor. The meadows had to be mowed twice each year, the first mowing when the grass had grown maybe a foot tall. This first harvest produced the major portion of the hay that was needed for the winter when the cows were confined to the stable and could not graze. There was a second mowing during the last part of summer, with a shorter growth that produced a finer and nutritionally richer hay, called *Grumet*, and both were given to the cows at the same feeding, a large portion of the rougher hay, a small portion of *Grumet*, like entrée and dessert. No additional feed, such as the cubes American farmers offer their cattle, was available. When it was ready to bring in, the mowed hay had to be raked into rows, and the rows into piles. These were loaded with a fork onto the flat trailer, where a worker placed it strategically to create a large and stable load. In the hay loft, our farmer, like most of the others, had an electric system that grabbed large amounts of hay with a pair of big metal claws and then carried it on a track to a part where it would be dropped for storage. We kids loved to jump into the mountain of hay and burrow channels and little chambers where we could hide or hang out.

Having dairy cattle was and is a commitment. They must be milked twice a day, and in those days the milking was done by hand. Cows, like human females, are endowed by their maker differently. Some have small, firm udders and others are weighed down by heavy bags. To my surprise, I learned that the size of the udder does not affect the amount of milk a cow will produce. A cow is most productive after she has given birth to a calf. A cow is usually milked by the same person every time, and the two know each other. The milker gives the cow a friendly pat on the rump, which she acknowledges by turning around to look. Then the milker sits down on a short three-legged stool, always on the right side. The udder gets wiped off with a damp cloth, and the process begins, two teats at a time, the stream of milk directed into a small bucket held between the knees. This would be the time when Grey, the old cat that was well-regarded by the family for her prowess as a mouser, would come hanging around. She would open her mouth, and a milker would direct the stream at her.

As I write these memories, I sometimes talk about them with my brother, Micky. He laughed when I told him about the cat, and he told me, news to me, that he, four or maybe five years old, would also open his mouth, imitating the cat, and would also get a squirt of cow-warm milk.

Everybody worked, even I, especially when a thunderstorm was brewing and a field of hay had to be raked and brought into the barn quickly before the downpour started. My mother soon learned to milk cows by hand and was assigned a couple to milk mornings and evenings. That was good for a daily pitcher of milk. I, too, learned to help with the animals. There were few fences then and a lot of the time the cows had to be watched during their grazing, boring work that belonged to children. I often helped by just keeping them company and I remember well how stiff and cold my naked feet would feel early in the morning when the dew on the grass felt freezing cold. I was also given responsibility for raising a calf now and then, when they had been weaned from the cow but were not yet ready to graze. At milking time, I would be given a bucket of milk for my calf and, submerging my hand in it, would let the calf suck on two fingers.

As we started to explore our new world, we found all kinds of food growing wild in the woods that surrounded our hamlet: tiny, delicious wild strawberries, raspberries, blueberries, beechnuts, and a great variety of wild mushrooms. All these soon became an important part of our daily meals, and what was not consumed right away was strung on thread into garlands and dried for the winter. My mother, always a magician at making a lot out of a little, made a delicious mushroom ragout, mushroom soup, and mushroom pickles, and, no matter what anybody else may claim, it was she who, back then, invented the veggie burger.

One day my mother came home elated from a trip into the woods. In addition to the usual mushrooms, she brought home an egg. She had been foraging when she saw a fox trotting toward the woods from the village. In its mouth was an egg. Without thinking, my mother set down her basket and chased the fox and, a small miracle, the fox dropped the egg and, another small miracle, the egg did not break. This story, unfortunately, has a sad ending. Both my brother and I clamored for the egg. After some agonizing, my mother decided that the little one needed it most and she fed the egg to my brother. Within minutes, Micky threw up the egg, and this made all three of us cry.

You may remember that on our first day in Enisried we were eating a breakfast of stolen eggs, and the justification my Aunt Erna gave. My mother gave us regular reminders of her way of thinking. When she came back from one of her foraging walks through the woods, whether I was along or not, she would take a little rest and sit down, always at the edge of a potato field. In the evening when we sat down to eat our mushroom dinner, there would also be a potato on our plate. I love potatoes to this day. To keep us from fighting over food, my mother devised a method to divide food between us, which she called *Christlich teilen*, dividing or sharing like Christians. The German language uses the same word for both dividing and sharing. If there was something good to eat, and naturally both my brother and I wanted it, she would let one of us cut it in two, but the other got first pick.

At first, I went out foraging with my mother, but more and more, I went out by myself. There was no danger, and I got a lot of satisfaction from providing a substantial portion of our daily diet. I got good at finding more and better mushrooms and berries than anyone else, and I jealously kept my places secret. Siegi, the younger of the two daughters, asked me several times to take her along when I went out. I told her to meet me in ten minutes at the front door and I slipped out the back door. After a couple of attempts to join me, she figured out that I wanted to go alone, and she gave up. Spending so much time in the woods, I came to believe for a while that I had extraordinary powers of will, maybe even supernatural ones, as I roamed through the sacred space of the woods in an exalted mixture of nature worship and my idea of Catholicism. I never told anyone, carefully guarding the secret of my powers, and later, when I was thirteen and we moved to Speyer, a city and away from my beloved woods, it became painfully clear to me that I was, after all, only a very ordinary girl.

Besides gathering food in the woods, another way for me to contribute to our meals was a matter of just plain luck. We children roamed all over the place and sometimes I would find in the tall grass or in the hayloft a clutch of eggs that some sneaky chicken had hidden, planning to hatch them. Of course, such illicit nests had to be turned in to the farmer's wife. But the honest finder would always be rewarded with a couple of the eggs. I can still remember how good it felt to run home and present them to my mother.

If we suffered from a lack of food on the farm, hunger was an even greater problem in the city. Townspeople came to our village daily. They arrived by train and walked up to our hamlet from the stop, a good mile away. Then they would go from house to house and simply beg for something edible. We called them "hamsterers" (not hamsters), and their activity was "hamstering." Sometimes they would have some things of small value to barter. At our house, the farmer's wife, who had been in service in the city as a young girl, always gave something. Herr Kugler, her husband, our landlord, kept a few colonies of bees in his small orchard. I remember once that a mouse had drowned in a jar of honey stored on a shelf in the basement. Frau Kugler fished the dead mouse out and gave the jar of honey to the next hamsterer who knocked on her door. That person could hardly believe the good luck and should have known that something was fishy.

My father came to visit us in Enisried only once. It must have been difficult for him. Not only was the distance between him and us great, but he and we also lived in different zones, we in the American-occupied one and he in the Russian one. Crossing from the Russian zone to a western one was illegal and dangerous. I do not know how much warning my mother had—I think he had written a letter—or how welcoming she felt and acted, but when he arrived, all three of us were shy around him. We had not seen him for several years. Little Micky hid under the table. My father came, just like a hamsterer, with a rucksack that contained not only clean clothes for a change, but also things to barter for food. The east and north of Germany had always been the industrial part of the country, and the south and west were more agricultural. In the Russian zone only a few manufacturing facilities had escaped destruction by bombs. Those were dismantled and shipped to Russia along the railroad tracks that had served for the delivery of materials and distribution of the finished goods. The region where my father now lived had once been the center for luxury goods like cameras and medical-optical equipment. The things he brought were much more modest, especially good fishing hooks and lures. All we had had up to then was rusty old hooks or even a bent-over straight pin on which a worm would be impaled.

Good at business, he traded these things in the village, going house to house, and soon his rucksack was filled with food, the prize being a large ham. My mother would bitterly recall and retell for the rest of her life that for our last meal together before he returned to his home, he cut a few slices off that ham to add to her offerings. The rest went back into his rucksack, along with what else he had been able to gather. I have a photograph that my father took of me during the few days of his visit, on a long walk through snow-covered woods. Micky is not in the picture; likely he was too small for a long hike. I do not remember what we talked about. Although my father's reputation for being tight-fisted was confirmed by his not sharing the contents of his rucksack, he was a conscientious provider after the divorce. The monthly postal transfer for child support was never a day late, and birthdays and Christmas were not forgotten. Later, after he, too, had settled in the "West" in the important commercial port city of Bremen, there was also an open invitation for Micky and me to spend our summer vacations with him. By then, he lived with the widow of a German officer, whom we were asked to call Aunt Mucky. She had a son about Micky's age and was kind to us. My brother usually spent at least a part of his vacation with our father. By then, I was in my teens and preferred to stay at home and find some kind of summer job to earn a little money.

During the war years as a young and rising star of the German industry, my father had plowed his profits back into the business without concern for his old age. All of that was lost because of Germany's defeat. He would never be self-employed again but worked on salary providing engineering services to shipbuilding concerns. On one of my visits as a young adult, he invited me to accompany him to the launch of a large ship, a very exciting experience. A bottle of champagne was smashed on the ship's bow and more bottles were drunk to celebrate the launch.

Now he felt he had to make up for the lost time and provide for his old age by means of additional contributions to his retirement account, the equivalent of our Social Security system. That was why he felt he could not afford to help me with my university education expenses. Sadly, he would not live long enough to retire but died at the age of sixty-four from a stroke on a business trip. My brother and I had both emigrated to the US by then and neither of us could reach Germany in time to attend his funeral. My mother attended, representing all three of us. Although divorced for many years by then, she never took off her wedding ring. I left it on her hand when she died, but it was handed to me along with her ashes. I now wear it alongside my own.

The last time I saw my father was during a prolonged visit to Germany before either of my children was old enough to attend school. He invited the three of us (their father was deployed in Korea) for a two-week vacation with him in his and Mucky's

Bremen flat and at a summer apartment he owned or rented, some distance from Bremen in a small town. Aunt Mucky did not come with us to the summer getaway. My father had been captured by the Russians but had been traded to the British and was interned in a prisoner-of-war camp for a couple of years. He had high regard for the British thereafter for the gentlemanly treatment he had received during his captivity. He enjoyed speaking English with my children. One of my fondest memories of him is of watching the three of them stride through a park, singing "Old McDonald Had a Farm" at the top of their voices.

On his single visit to us in Enisried, one fundamental disagreement between my parents at this important juncture in their lives was my father's expectation that we would join him in the Russian zone. He had engineering work opportunities, which were totally lacking in south-eastern Bavaria. My mother, even though she had never been vocal or informed about ideology or politics, had taken an incredibly courageous leap of faith so that we could live in a noncommunist part of Germany. For this and for other personal reasons, she liked her new surroundings despite the deprivations of our situation. By then she was in a relationship with the young dairy manager. As it turned out, my father was in a relationship, too, and had been living with Mucky for some time.

My mother worked hard from morning to night to provide for us. After the day's work, she would go out dancing. She had fun and was in charge of her own life. I remember watching her one evening as she got ready for a fancy-dress dance during carnival time. She was tacking a silver crescent moon and gold-colored stars on a beautiful dark blue silk dress from the old days. With a little glitter in her hair, she disappeared from our view on the back of a motorcycle with her silk skirt billowing, dressed up as the Queen of the Night. But everything in life has its price. On her night out, I was not allowed to sleep with the farmer's daughters upstairs but in our own little room so that little Micky would not be alone. My mother was crushed to hear in the morning that he had risen from his bed in the middle of the night, screaming from a nightmare. His eyes were wide open, but he would not react to my entreaties to be quiet. He woke up the whole house. Our landlords did not come down to my assistance, although I imagine that they knew that our mother had gone out. They told us in the morning that they had prayed for us. Micky's nightmares were almost certainly caused by the trauma we all had lived through. Today I know that I had been harmed, too. While I was able to sleep well, I was paralyzed by fear when I was awake and alone. Often the girls got up early while I was still asleep. I remember terrible anxiety, afraid to stay there alone, afraid to get out of bed. If the old dog, Karo, barked, I imagined that it was at robbers or murderers. If he did not bark, I was afraid that he had been silenced. It took me years to get over such fears.

There was little privacy for either landlords or tenants, living so closely together. We shared the Kugler family's house, living in that back room, for close to five years. My mother assisted the farmer's wife and later Annie, her older daughter, with cooking and baking on many special and not so special occasions. They worked side-by-side in the hayfield and the cow stable, but they never dropped the formal address in their interaction. To the last day, they remained "Frau Janiel" (my mother) and "Herr und Frau Kugler" (our landlords).

My mother's incredible fashion sense and her ability to sew and do any kind of needlework soon made her a very valued member of the community. After six years of rationing, when all materials were diverted to the war effort, there was a long-pent-up appetite for new clothes. At first, there was nothing to be had in the stores. My mother had an uncanny ability to duplicate any garment from a picture in a fashion magazine, making up her own pattern for it. She would receive payment in the form of food, or sometimes firewood or blocks of dried peat. Unfortunately, she was a terrible businesswoman. Seeing the picture of a gorgeous professional model wearing a certain garment gives the viewer the illusion that this garment would make her look gorgeous, too. That was clearly not going to happen for these sturdy country women. It never occurred to her to have an upfront agreement as to what and how much her compensation would be when she completed a dress. She managed to keep us fed, nevertheless. I did not own a large wardrobe, and everything I wore was made by my mother. I liked my clothes fitting snugly. My mother wanted them to be ample to give me room to grow in. So when we had the final fitting, I would breathe out and then suck in my tummy and not breathe to be as slim as possible. But my mother got wise to my attempt to cheat and, just taking her time until I had to breathe again, she ruined my ploy. Mom had the bad habit when she did a fitting of holding straight pins between her lips for want of a third hand. One time when my Aunt Erna said something funny and made my mother laugh, she swallowed one. I think that had to have happened earlier in Jägerndorf, (today Krnov), because she was taken to a doctor right away, and he was able to remove it. Sadly, she was not the only one to have this foolish habit. Much later I learned that Maria, my aunt Mimi's young maid, also accidentally swallowed a needle or pin, but she was too embarrassed or afraid to tell anyone, and the thing stayed in her body and travelled until it reached her heart, and she died. Well, that is the story we were told.

There was a hierarchy in the village. Importance depended on wealth. The Settele family living smack in the center of the hamlet were clearly head and shoulders above the other folk. Theirs was a large house. They owned a tractor before anyone else had one and they had the only telephone in the hamlet, which they generously made available for emergencies. As good Catholics, they had almost life-size statues of saints in their house and they also had many children, I think six, the youngest being Klara, my classmate. Their children had access to education if they wanted it. One of Klara's older sisters was a teacher. One of her brothers would go to high school but did not go on to college.

One way to measure the wealth of a family was to count their cattle. Our landlords, the Kugler family, were a little above average with about eighteen to twenty cows. They also stood out because they had a couple of horses and a little trailer, outfitted to carry the barrel in which they delivered the daily milk, morning and evening, to the dairy. A couple of other families had horses. Some brought their milk in a contraption pulled by a steer or cow. The poorest, who had less milk to carry, brought theirs in a hutch on the farmer's own back.

Our hamlet was then a place without young men. The ones who would eventually come home from the war had not yet done so. Almost all the men in the hamlet were older and married. There was one notable exception. The only store or business was the dairy, or, more precisely, the cheese kitchen, in the center, right next to the little chapel. Mornings and evenings after the milking, all the farmers delivered their milk there to be weighed and recorded. Every now and then a woman from the equivalent of the health department came to test the milk to make sure that it had not been diluted with water. Aunt Erna dubbed her the Milk Goat. Several days a week, maybe all weekdays, in the large copper kettle in the middle of the cheese kitchen, the milk would be boiled, rennet was added to make it coagulate, and a huge new wheel of Emmental cheese was started by sweeping up the curd with a large net and filling it into a wooden form. The master of this important enterprise was a young man with tightly curled, dark red hair, big white teeth in a mouth that loved to laugh, and freckles all over his face and arms. He could yodel, sing, and especially dance with a lot of gusto. Moreover, he owned a motorcycle. He was the target of the dreams and schemes of all the unmarried girls, who regularly supplied him with edible treats. In this staunchly Catholic part of Bavaria, it was then customary that a girl would try to find a good husband and when this did not happen and all hope had evaporated, she would go into a cloister to become a nun, a bride of Christ.

My mother was by far the most exotic bird, not just in the hamlet, but probably in the surroundings. Soon the dairyman started to court her. He was really kind to us children, too. I was torn between liking him for his good looks and the good things he would bring when he came to visit, and jealousy of my mother's attention and her lack of loyalty to my absent father. This also was the time when preparing for my first communion had begun. All the kids in my first communion class, including myself, got very serious about our commitment to the Catholic Church and we constantly competed with one another in being holier than thou. Every one of the other children had a patron saint after whom they were named, and it was their name-day rather than their birthday that was celebrated. "After all," they would say to me, "even a dog has a birthday." I was the only child who had a heathen name; a fact that was often pointed out to me. In the weeks before First Communion, we were all terribly nervous about getting it just right when the big day would arrive. For instance, we asked each other how grave a sin it would be if the host touched our teeth or, God forbid, one should even bite down on it by mistake?

Inspired by the stories of sainted martyrs who had endured all sorts of torture for staying true to their faith, stories for all to see in the statues and paintings in the richly decorated baroque church, we were wondering how strong our own commitment might be if it were ever tested. I remember when one of my little friends posed to the rest of us the question of what sacrifice we might be prepared to make to be permitted to take communion. In the end, we all agreed that we would even swallow a dead mouse, if necessary. Luckily, nothing more serious than abstaining from food and drink during the entire morning, including a three-mile walk to our communion mass, would ever be required of us.

Religion and the promise to go to heaven were constantly on our minds. By then, my parents either had already been divorced or were getting divorced, not an entirely easy process at the time. There had to be an insurmountable obstacle to the continuation of the marriage; I suppose it would typically have been infidelity. It was shameful and deemed a great disadvantage to be declared the guilty party. Not only was I sad and disappointed that God failed to hear my fervent prayers for my parents' reconciliation, but my little friends would also innocently rub salt into my wounds when they told me how sorry they felt for me since I could not hope to find my parents in heaven after all our deaths.

But before the first communion came the first confession, about which I had a particular reason to be nervous. As the youngest of the three girls in our household and with the lower status accorded to a refugee child, I was always assigned the least desirable role in our make-believe games. While Anni and Siegi appointed themselves my parents or some other authority figures, I was cast as the hapless daughter who had gotten pregnant out of wedlock. To make the game even more realistic, they made me stuff a pillow under my dress. My unfortunate situation was then discovered by my make-believe elders, and I was properly chastised for my wrongdoing. As the dreaded day of my real-life confession came closer and closer, I worried about it all the time. When I finally was in the confessional, I was so nervous that I could not remember the order of the ten commandments. The priest, who I was sure recognized me from communion preparation class, had to help me by asking me about my sins, commandment by commandment. When he got to the sixth, as I knew he would sooner or later, and he asked me if I had committed lewd acts, I knew that because of our games, I had to say "yes." But I was really devastated when he went on to ask, "alone or with others?" Without a chance of explaining that Annie and Siegi had made me do it, I had to say, "with others."

For my communion my mother had made my dress out of

pieces of silk from a parachute that had been found in the fields. The farmer's wife contributed a large, partially used candle from one of her girls' first communion. Unfortunately, no one had any white shoes I could wear. In the end, my mother sewed shoes for me from a scrap of sailcloth. But what to do about the soles? After much agonizing, Aunt Erna came up with the solution. She cut out a piece of the linoleum flooring in her movie theater from under a seat in the last row, where it would not show, and my mother fashioned soles and glued them to the shoes. Then she made them sparkling white by brushing them with toothpaste.

Neither my mother nor my Aunt Erna ever went to church. Moreover, they made disparaging remarks about the fat priest, the subservient, bitter and exploited nuns, and the local farmers who were so pious but at the same time often stingy and petty. Though Aunt Erna made no apologies, my mother protested that she would love to go to church but, alas, could not, as the incense made her faint. I was embarrassed for my family in front of my devout little classmates, who all had proper parents. I worried about the prospects for my mother's and Aunt Erna's eternal souls. For the celebration of my first communion, my mother did go to church with me, and she lasted through the long service without fainting, holy smoke notwithstanding.

I remember one special day in school, when each child was given a little tube of toothpaste and a new toothbrush from, I believe, a UNICEF donation. On the walk home, we all tasted the toothpaste, and we found it delicious, so different from the bland, chalky stuff we used. We took one little lick and then another. I think that all of us had eaten the entire little tubes long before we got home. Later, also from UNICEF funds, refugee children received lunch at school. Most often, it was a kind of soupy concoction in which noodles and clumps of powdered egg were prominent, but sometimes we got a bread roll and a cup of hot chocolate. As a special treat, once in a great while, we even received half a bar of chocolate instead of the cocoa. A meal for a school child was a real boost to the nutrition of a refugee family. When the lunch program continued even during the summer vacation, we took turns walking three miles each way with milk cans to collect the food for ourselves and for each other.

This was one of the few times when we had an advantage over the farm kids. More often, we refugee kids felt like children of a lesser god. All the farms had a house name by which the families were known in the region, a name that seldom gave a clue as to its origin. For instance, the real name of our host family was Kugler, but everyone knew them as the Gellers. Frau Kugler was Mother Geller; Herr Kugler was Father Geller. When adults wanted to initiate a conversation with a schoolchild, they would ask not, "What is your name?" but "To whom do you belong?" The formula for the child's answer was "I belong to the Gellers," or whatever the house name was. We refugee children, of course, had no such house names. I remember the pain it gave me to have to answer on such occasions that we were "only refugees."

Like farm children everywhere, the children of my village were expected to help with the chores; some work was considered children's work. You may remember I mentioned cow herding. During the summer, when the dairy cows spent their entire day grazing in the lush and juicy pastures, I spent many hours with the younger of our landlords' daughters, Siegi, watching cows eat grass. From my father, I had received a box of pastel chalks and some pads of newsprint. Siegi and I would entertain ourselves by sketching, somewhat competitively, the world around us, both eventually becoming pretty good at it. Other chores for children were gathering the fallen apples in the orchard and cranking the handle of the centrifuge when the honey was harvested in the spring and in the fall, interesting changes from the quiet country life with the added incentive of sweet, edible rewards. Seppl, from the age of about eleven or twelve, drove the tractor that had recently been acquired. Once, he got off the tractor while it was still running, and the heavy machine backed over him, breaking his collarbone.

I remember the farmer's daughters and myself being "allowed" to roll cigars for their dad out of tobacco leaves from a small tobacco patch that he had planted. We were instructed to make long and thin cigars, which he called "bichinies," a corruption of "Virginias," and which he remembered fondly from the days before the war, when the real thing could be bought in a store. The supple leaves had been cured in one of many experimental ways with plum juice or tea or similar substances. We wound them around a thin hollow stem of grass. Competing against each other for the farmer's coveted praise, we turned out some decent cigars.

Next to tobacco, the vice most painfully missed was the drinking of alcohol. Hard liquor was not available during the first years after the war to anyone who did not have direct contact with American military personnel, contact that did not extend beyond the larger cities. My Aunt Erna somehow came into possession of an old distilling apparatus and the plot was hatched that for the next New Year's Eve, she would produce alcohol. The farmer gladly participated in this plan and planted a patch of sugar beets. These were scrubbed and maybe peeled, then cut and boiled in the copper kettle usually reserved for boiling laundry. The liquid was squeezed out by pushing the pulp through a sieve. This juice was boiled, and eventually a clear liquid started dripping from the end of the coiled copper tubing. Information for doing such procedures correctly was not available. The product tasted so awful that none of the adults was able to drink it. We children somehow got hold of some of this concoction. Either pretending to be, or really being tipsy, we ran around in the crunchy snow that covered the moonlit yard, laughing and yelling. I remember getting sick to my stomach and vomiting before my mother packed me into my bed.

Occasions of that sort, with unhappy outcomes for children, were the exception. For the most part we had a close and happy family life. Interaction between my mother and my brother and me was different from the interaction between the typical local parents and their children. Herr and Frau Kugler hardly talked to their kids, unless it was to assign a task or to issue a mild rebuke. Some of my friends, who were at the tail-end of a long string of offspring, even addressed their parents with the formal *Ihr* (thou) rather than the familiar *Du* (you). My mother did everything with us. During one long winter, we—mostly she and I, since Micky was still too small—created a whole nativity scene from papier-mâché, which we made ourselves from shredded newspaper and a little flour and water on self-made wire figures, with real hair (ours), beards of sheep fur and clothes from scraps of cloth. (My mother had lots of those.) This included not only the holy family but also kings with gifts and shepherds with sheep and cow and donkey, and a manger. The scene got larger and larger as the winter went on, and everything had to be made from what we could find in and around the house. The hobby shop did not yet exist in Germany.

It was my mother who taught all of us to ice skate on the pond just outside our house and who taught all the kids in the house and our friends the basic steps of the then-popular dances: Vienna waltz, polka, foxtrot and schottische, tango. Our studio was the floor of the large hay-barn, and while she was dancing with one of us, the rest would practice with a broom for a partner. For sure, it was not all fun for her. I gave her a big scare once when I, being alone and bored one afternoon, decided to entertain myself by riding a wooden handcart down the ramp that led to the hay barn. At first, I went down sitting in the cart. Then I decided to try it standing up. When I could not control the steering and tumbled down the steep side of the ramp, cart and I rolling several times, my left arm was knocked out of its elbow joint. With enormous pain it now dangled much longer than normal in the sleeve of my long-sleeved shirt. I ran into the house yelling, "My arm is off! My arm is off!" After my mother calmed me down and laid me on her bed, she had to walk into the village to call, from the Settele telephone, the doctor in the next town. He was out making his rounds, but somehow his wife knew how to get messages to him. By the time he arrived at our house, it was evening and my arm had swollen to a multiple of its normal size. To anesthetize me so he could set it properly, he put a wad of gauze on my face and started to drip ether from a hand-held bottle while I counted backward from twenty. I only got to sixteen.

Apart from some short hysterical outbursts, my mother held up under these challenges astoundingly well most of the time, but I know now that there were times when she must have felt overwhelmed. I remember one evening, maybe it was at the end of a rainy day, when the three of us had been cooped up in our single room with Micky and me squabbling all day while she tried to work. Suddenly, she left the room in exasperation. When I went to look for her, I found her crying outside, sitting in the dark on our stack of cut wood.

Another instance occurred when my mother went behind the house, where the land rose steeply up a hill. There Herr Kugler had planted an orchard of fruit trees and among them he had a bee house with a couple of colonies of bees for pollination. I don't know why my mother went there, maybe to look for a fallen apple. Some of the bees attacked her and she was stung several times. To make matters even worse, in her distress she lost her balance and fell on the rough terrain, suffering some bloody scrapes and bruises.

The old farmhouse where we lived had two sources of heat during the winter, not counting the cannon stove in our little room. One was the kitchen range where a wood-and-peat fire was built and lit every morning, summer and winter, for cooking and for providing a supply of hot water for dishes and personal hygiene. The other was a green tile stove with a footprint of at least five-by-five feet and at least six-feet tall. It was built into one corner of the large living room and had two open sides surrounded by a bench, which provided a fine place to huddle with something to read. The coffered ceiling of the living room had been made by a carpenter a hundred years earlier, probably from fresh wood. As the wood dried it shrank and the seams between the boards opened into narrow cracks. In the wintertime, there would be little mouse tails hanging in rows from these cracks in the ceiling above and around the warm stove. We kids would climb onto the bench and grab the tip of a mouse tail in each hand, with the owners of the tails squeaking and tugging and eventually pulling free.

Another source of heat for the downstairs was animal warmth from the cows in the stable. They spent all day and all night during the long winter months eating the hay that had been gathered during the summertime. The second floor, where the bedrooms were located, had no heat at all. The beds were punishingly cold. It would take a long time lying there, curled up into a tight ball, before one could get warm enough to relax and hope to fall asleep. For this reason, we kids procured a brick each, not an easy feat, which we warmed on the stove during the evening, wrapped into a towel and took with us when we went upstairs to bed. In the mornings, we would put our clothes on under our bed covers.

While our life could never return to the intended, old "normal," it did, over time, change to a new kind of normal. We made some friends with other refugee families and among the locals. Somewhere we acquired a black kitten. Later, when Micky must have been about school age, he asked my mother if he could bring home a young bird. Mother agreed that he might, but only if the bird had fallen out of its nest and had been abandoned by its parents. Imagine the lucky coincidence that a baby raven, or maybe a crow, fell out of its nest the next day and Micky happened to be there and brought it home. The little thing could not have been more than a few days old. It could barely rise on its legs. Its feathers were still little pins. Every time someone came near the shoebox that served as its nest, it opened a huge yellow mouth and

demanded to be fed. But what to feed it? He ate just about everything, but he was especially fond of meat, which we rarely saw on
our own plates, even in tiny portions. So on the long way home
from school, I now kept a sharp eye out for little bugs and earth-
worms, carrying them home in my pockets for the ever-hungry bird.
I was just reading *Huckleberry Finn* and *Tom Sawyer* in German,
and we called the bird "Huck." When Hucky outgrew his shoebox,
he was all over the room, hiding macaroni and other tidbits behind
the cushions for future reference and a cold surprise for anyone
sitting down with bare legs. At night, he slept on the back of a chair
with a piece of newspaper on the floor, for he had very efficient
digestion.

One day, my mother went on a bus trip to a popular excursion
destination just across the border into Austria. To bribe us to stay at
home without complaint, she allowed us to skip school that day.
Somehow, she had managed to procure a bag of dark cherries for us.
Micky and I stayed in the room all day, mostly in my mother's bed,
and we played with the bird and ate cherries. You can hardly
imagine the distress my mother showed at the sight that greeted her
when she returned home from her excursion in the evening. Every
surface and all the linens had big dark cherry stains.

Hucky was a cute pet and with my help soon learned to fly,
figuring out on his own how to lift into the air and land on a low
branch or on the roof of the house. But with no parents to show
him, he did not know how to fly down. We had to get a ladder, and
between Seppl and me we gently tossed him into the air until he
got it. He became a good flyer and would frequently land on our
shoulders. Now when we walked to the village to visit friends, our
black kitten would follow us like a puppy, and Hucky followed in
the air. Somewhere they waited, and on our return home they both
suddenly showed up and accompanied us again. We loved that bird
so much and were devastated when one evening he failed to come
home. We could not find him anywhere. Later we learned that

while we were at school, he had flown over to a field where a family was taking a break from their work to have a mid-morning snack. Used to getting handouts, he begged for food and was killed with a rake for no reason at all, just as Texans are wont to kill any snake they encounter, poisonous or not.

I was an avid reader, but there was little to read. *Tom Sawyer*, on loan to me from a friend, was printed on loose leaf newsprint in newspaper format. My mother could not take books when we fled, and new ones were not available. We passed books around or, during the train ride to school and home or sat side by side and shared a book. Most likely we would get hold of a book by Karl May (1842-1912), a prolific German fiction writer of fat tomes. He became and perhaps still is the most-read German author. About half his stories are set in the American Old West, the central figures being Chief Winnetou and Old Shatterhand (Karl himself, glorified) and the rest in an imaginary land in the Middle East, featuring Kara Ben Nemsi (Karl again) and his funny sidekick, Hadji Halef Omar. Despite detailed description of his locations, he never visited America or the Middle East.

In a little cupboard in the farmhouse's living room were only a handful of books. When I got desperate, I would go back to the only one that held any interest for me, one about missionary work in Africa. I tolerated the religious stuff and concentrated on the description of African places and people. One day when Seppl let me follow him into the attic, I struck gold. I found close to a hundred little paper-bound booklets, episodes in a subscription series from the early 1900s, judging by the graphics of the cover. The eponymous title was *Rigo Muratti, Genannt der Schwarze Rigo* (called Black Rigo). The hero was a Tarzan-like superman in love with a blond and sweet woman, whom I shall call Roselind, and pursued by the ruthlessly smitten daughter of a rich *haciendero*, Mercedes Brombilla. Rigo wanted nothing more than to swing through the vines in his jungle and cuddle with Roselind, but the hot-blooded Mercedes would not have that and set nasty traps for him. The small booklets each had maybe twenty or thirty pages that were full of excitement. Each one would end with Rigo being in mortal danger—say, having to jump out of a third-floor window—and the next issue would pick up with a deep sigh of relief over a close escape, such as, "Luckily just then a truck passed by loaded with banana leaves."

Television was still many years away in Germany. Besides the radio, illustrated magazines were popular there, as they were in the US. But they were expensive and not available in our hamlet or in the surrounding region. Somebody had a clever idea: subscribe to a bundle of five or six different magazines and keep them for a week. They were delivered by bicycle and exchanged for new issues. The rate of the subscription was highest when they were newly issued and went down as they were getting older each week. My mother and I enjoyed the magazines, especially the ones about fashion. Some had literary content, others focused on news and politics. I remember the novel *Hotel Shanghai* by Vicki Baum, published in segments, the first piece of adult fiction that my mother allowed me to read. From it I learned that literature can transport the reader from modest circumstances to interesting far places, and that book helped make me a world traveler for life.

One Sunday afternoon, my mother and I were lounging, had likely enjoyed a cup of coffee and a little slice of cake and now were reading from our bundle. One of us noticed a little mouse under the table. She was finding crumbs and was so cute, sitting up on her haunches as she nibbled. We were both very still so as not to scare her and kept watching her for a long time. That night my mother set a trap. Later, when I said I hoped the mouse would visit again, I was told that she had been caught and was dead. My mother made sure I did not see the little corpse.

I can't remember when or how a Sears, Roebuck mail-order catalogue fell into my hands. WOW! Now I knew what Alice felt when she landed in Wonderland. This was proof that America really was the land of unlimited possibilities. Here the challenge was not how to get what you needed—who said needed?—but what you *wanted*. Here the hard part was what to choose from seemingly endless options. I spent many hours looking at the thick book, cover to cover, and never got over my amazement. What I was not prepared for and did not understand was the power of American marketing. I learned that the hard way. Much later, during my then husband's and my first weeks in Charleston, S.C., we bought, on my initiative, a forty-volume *Encyclopedia Britannica*, when what we really needed was a window air-conditioning unit for our sweltering little rented house. But back to Enisried.

There were two so-called swimming holes in the little creek that ran near our hamlet, modestly designated boys' bath and girls' bath, a mile or two distant from one another. We went to the girls' bath once and it was not very nice. Here the creek flowed through a meadow between tall banks and was only about waist deep, not enough for swimming. We had to stand and crouch down to get all wet. The boys' bath, on the other hand, was right above the house that used to be a mill and was still called *Obermühle* (upper mill). Here the creek, where it had once driven a wheel, was wider and deeper. While it certainly could not be called a pool, it was large enough for several people to be in at the same time and to swim a few strokes. This is where we all taught ourselves to swim. The first step was to do the dead man's float, holding one's breath, face down. The next was to try floating on one's back with eyes open. When we could swim a few strokes, we sometimes hiked or biked to ponds in the region. We refugees were mostly city folk with much looser customs about the separation or interaction between the sexes. So the much better boys' bath was soon integrated and eventually even the local kids all came there, too. I think the local adults gave up swimming altogether.

There were other customs that bit the dust as a direct consequence of the refugees' arrival. Since time immemorial, on December 6, St. Nicolas Day, the teenage and young adult boys of the village would cover themselves with old rags and cast-off clothes, worn inside out, with chains and cowbells for belts. Over their heads they pulled a sack with slits to see through. There would be four or five of them—all the young adult boys there were in the hamlet. After dark, they would go to each house with kids and, not knocking, burst inside with a fearful noise. They would go from room to room, threatening and commanding everybody to pray.

A long tradition for the locals, the whole thing was a total surprise to us refugees. The first time we experienced it, I started reciting the Lord's Prayer before they had all entered the room, and even my mother fell in with me while little Micky screamed in terror. The next year, we knew what to expect and I had braced myself for it. After all, we knew quite well who the boys were, even though we could not recognize them individually. My mother kept a keen eye on the path from the village center to our house, and when she saw them approach, she told Micky to hide inside our wardrobe and be very still until they had gone away again. They hollered, stomped their feet, rattled their chains and clanged their bells, but I was determined that I would not pray for them. So in the end, they grabbed me by the wrists and pulled me with them as they left the house. They stomped through the crunchy snow in the direction of the woods, dragging me along. Every now and then, they would stop and shout at me to start praying. More and more stubbornly, I shook my head in refusal. Now and then, one of them would pull off a mitten and run his finger under my eyes. But, no, I was not crying, not yet. For the teasing I knew would follow, crying would be worse than praying. After a while, we arrived at a shed at the edge of the woods, and they roughly pushed me inside and made a noisy show of chaining and locking the door. I was able to hold panic at bay, even as I heard them stomping away. Sure enough, after a little while, they came back and grudgingly pulled me out, and as a wave of relief washed over me, I finally prayed.

Coming home, I found my mother in tears and near panic. In her anxiety, she had hidden the key to the wardrobe and now could not remember where. Again and again, she would call to Micky to respond to her to make sure he had not suffocated inside the wardrobe. His little voice would answer, asking her if the "Clauses" had gone away. Finally, she found the key and Micky came out of the wardrobe. This would be the last time the Clauses had their fun in our village. It turned out that others had not fared as well as we. Freddy, a refugee boy of middle school age, the son of friends of ours, who was always getting in trouble because of his smart-alecky ways, was badly beaten up that night, seriously enough for his parents to have to take him to a doctor the next morning. But there was even worse. The Clauses also had dragged Annie, the teenage oldest daughter of our landlord, with them and apparently there had been some groping of the pretty girl. Nothing was said out loud, but there was a lot of whispering. My mother sat down with me and asked me to tell her exactly what had happened while I was in their hold. She was visibly relieved when I gave her a full account.

To be truthful, I liked to hang around the older boys, and liked the attention they gave me. Once in a long while they would ask if I, or we if we were in a group, wanted to ride on horseback as the horses were returned from the pasture to their stable. There were no saddles or tack. I can't remember how I mounted unless the guys helped me, but sitting on the bare back and holding on to the shaggy mane was exciting. I think the boys led the horses. Mostly the guys' attention came in the form of teasing. I did not have many clothes. One skirt, which I guess I wore often, was a design of my mother's and popular among her acquaintances. It was a half-circle of cloth, or rather two quarter-circles, with stitched accordion-fold pleats, narrow at the waist and broader at the bottom. I wore this skirt for a long time, and as I grew taller it fit more snugly at the waist and got shorter. The boys laughed and called it my lampshade skirt, and they told me to go away and come back when I was a thousand weeks old. I don't think I got it then, but if one does the math, it comes out to about twenty years. One of the younger boys, Wolfgang Settele, the one who gave me bicycle rides first and later motorcycle rides, stayed in touch with me over the years and sent Christmas messages when e-mail became available. The last time I was in Enisried, returning from a Graz wedding with a woman travel friend, I let him know ahead and he insisted that we drop in for an afternoon. He was married, of course. I knew his pretty wife, who had baked a lovely cherry cake for our visit. They lived in a nice house surrounded by a delightful garden, all well-kept. In the driveway was their big Mercedes-Benz. He had obviously been successful in his profession, business administration. He told us then that he was crediting me for his success. He said that after I had started Oberschule I once said to him, "You cannot go there, you are too dumb." He told me that after a couple of false starts he persevered, and eventually he found his niche. I do not remember saying those words, but he may be right.

During the summer, we would sometimes pack food for the day to take to a small lake, almost two hours' walk for us. We camped there from morning to night. Once, some ducks came floating by, and a friend who was with us caught two of them and wrung their necks. They were tied together and kept in the little stream that fed the lake to keep them fresh. Some hours later, on the other side of the lake, a farm wife came out calling for her fowl: Deedeedeedee! Deedeedeedee! That's when we understood why the ducks had been so easy to catch. The woman came over to ask us if we had seen them, but we were afraid and did not confess.

It was in this lake that I really taught myself to swim, after starting in the creek at the mill and, even though I never learned the

American crawl but only the breaststroke, I eventually became a pretty good swimmer.

A few years later Annie was old enough to be courted, but she was discreet. A nice young man, who was going to inherit his family's farm, came to call on her and he was always greeted by her parents and was always fed a meal that included two eggs sunny side up. They called that *Oxe Oge* (local dialect for *Ochsenaugen*: bullseyes). After the snack the family would withdraw from the living room to give the young couple some privacy. In due course, the two were married, but I no longer lived at the farm. Sadly, the marriage did not last long. Annie died young from cancer without ever having children.

In those days, Roma people—we called them Gypsies—still traveled in Germany in their little painted caravans, drawn by a team of tiny horses. Once or twice a year, two or three of these caravans would set up at the edge of the woods, some distance away from the hamlet. These were exciting interruptions of our boring routine for old and young alike. We were curious about these swarthy-skinned, strange folk in their colorful clothes, but we were also suspicious of them. We often forget the Roma when we remember the Holocaust. Hitler had vilified them, and many lost their lives in concentration camps. It was mostly their "otherness" that made us fearful. Everyone observed some common rules: don't hang laundry on the line and never give a Roma person an egg, as a death in the family would be sure to follow. Shame on us. How could we be so silly?

I remember a Roma woman coming to the house to ask for permission to fill her jug with water. We filled it for her, but she had to wait outside for us to bring it. Sometime later, we saw a small and harmless snake near the spot where she had waited for the water. We were absolutely convinced that there was a sinister connection to her earlier visit.

Sometimes these visitors in their caravans would invite the

villagers, by word of mouth, to a circus performance, which included their children, who were excellent acrobats and horseback riders. I remember going to a neighboring village for such an event on the crossbar of a bicycle, belonging to Wolfgang Settele, the boy who had his first crush on me. Skinny, barefoot, tanned, and wind-blown as I was, I did not look all that different from the Roma girls. As a matter of fact, a friend of my mother's later told her that a local woman sitting close to her on the grass watching the circus had pointed me out to her companion and had ventured the guess that I would probably be the next one to perform some amazing stunt.

Just as children living on a farm will observe how life begins, they will also be witnesses to life ending, sometimes associated with tenderness, other times with a shameful absence of feeling. Our farm wife, Frau Kugler, let her broody hens sit on clutches of their eggs, and in spring and early summer there often was one or some-times even more than one hen going around clucking and scratching in the dirt, followed by a flock of baby chicks trying to do everything she demonstrated. The law of averages dictates that approximately half of these chicks would turn out to be roosters. But a flock of chickens only needs one rooster, and the chicks' father already had that job. So once these young roosters grew to roasting size, they would go to the table one by one. The slaughter of a chicken is an ordinary event on a farm. I remember writing an essay for my German class, accompanied by a drawing, about our landlady plucking a chicken that was still alive. Even though I was just a kid, I called her out for this appalling cruelty, and she said that the feathers were just so much easier to pull out that way.

This reminds me of another time when, coming from the Bahtler farm at the center of the village, loud screaming attracted a growing number of rubberneckers, including me. The farmer and his wife were close to their back door with a pig, not quite fully grown, that squealed without pause in the most heartrending manner. It was on the ground on its side. The farmer's wife was holding it down, and her husband with a handful of hay was force-fully stroking the side of its belly from just under the neck to the tail. This went on for a long time, with the poor animal shrieking at full voice. The whispered consensus was that the creature had an obstruction in its digestive tract which they were trying to resolve. In the end, they shooed off the onlookers, and within a short time the screaming stopped.

It was not much later, on a day when we had had physical education at my school, in the gym—I cannot remember the exer-cises—that in the late afternoon I started feeling a bad pain in my lower belly that got sharper and sharper. All I could think about was that poor screaming pig and the bad end its story had taken. I knew I would not be killed, but I feared that I would die. I somehow got to the hospital in Füssen; I think my mother's boyfriend took me on his motorcycle. An appendectomy was performed, and there had been some complications that were explained to me as an entanglement in my intestines. I stayed in the hospital for about a week. I remember sharing the room with a local woman who was very funny, and that it was extremely painful for me to laugh. She made me laugh a lot.

A sad incident happened in a neighboring village. The stables in all the houses were built the same way, with a large tank below ground where the manure accumulated. Hay eaters' dung is not very smelly, and some ninety-nine percent of the contents of the tank below our house was cow waste. Once or twice a year the tanks had to be pumped out, and that was done by the owners. The smaller farms with only a few cows had a large barrel on wheels that a steer or cow or horse or tractor would pull, and they would spray this waste on a hay pasture to fertilize it. Our farmer had a system of pipes, a stack of them, maybe sixteen to twenty feet long, that could be connected to each other, the last segment fitted to something resembling a fire hose for discharging and fertilizing one area and then moving the pipes to another area to cover the meadow. That was done during the cold season when cows were not grazing, and I remember seeing the waste on top of patches of old snow. This work was in process at another farm in another village, where two brothers, refugees, were hired hands. The rumors had it that the pump failed and one of the brothers decided to descend into the tank to see if he could get it going again. When he did not return soon and did not respond to his brother's calling, the other one descended to see if he needed help and both brothers died from the noxious gases in that hellish pit.

This story brings to mind another accident, which may have been the result of nefarious action. There was a youngish man, a refugee, who was courting a pair of sisters, also refugees, in our village. He walked with a limp, and for some reason he was disliked by the local men. My mother told me that at dances he was bullied. He rode a motorcycle, and one day, motoring in the dark, he ran into a string of barbed wire that had been stretched across the road he was traveling. Luckily, he was wearing a leather motor bike jacket and although he was badly hurt, his injuries were not life-threatening. Whether somebody had set this trap, knowing that he would pass right there, or he was traveling where he should not have been, I never knew. There was occasional tension between "them and us," but mostly locals and new arrivals got along well enough.

A local family consisting of a young widow, her old mother, a little daughter about my age, and a hired hand, lived in the homestead known *as Obermühle*, next to our swimming hole. They lived the farthest from the village center by the road that led to the train station and to Seeg. The hired man would chase us when we, on the way home from school, stopped at the bridge over the mill stream to fish for the brook trout we could see in the clear water. The old grandmother of the child walked about dressed in tatters and looking like a witch. We never caught a trout, and we never missed the opportunity to throw a couple of rocks onto the family's shed roof before going on homeward. I think the prudish villagers suspected that something was going on between the young mother and the hired man. I hope there was. Later, long after I was already living in the US, somebody told me that the rift had been healed and the family was participating in the village community.

Speaking of trout, Aunt Erna's brother, Fred, an enthusiastic angler, came to visit her in Enisried. He and Aunt Erna arrived at our place when we were not at home, and they entered through an open window. Mother was embarrassed when we came home and found them there. They had tidied up and washed our dishes, which had only been stacked. He did not stay in our already crowded room but with a family with whom Aunt Erna was friendly. He spent hours at the brook, not intimidated by the hired man in the *Obermühle*. Fred did not fish with a hook. He used a snare, a sliding loop made from a violin string which he attached to the tip of his fishing pole. The trout, as well as a larger fish, I think pike, would shoot about in the crystal-clear water, and then suddenly stop and remain motionless for minutes at a time. How could they do it in the current? When Fred spied a fish so still, he would carefully insert the snare into the water in front of the fish's head, then past the head, and then pull the rod back fast. The loop tightened behind the head, and the fish was caught. Fred would toss it onto the grassy bank, where it would flop about until he put it out of its misery with his pocketknife. We kids were watching with a mixture of admiration and envy.

Our hamlet was only about thirty miles due north of the foot of the Alps. Every now and then, we would make an excursion to one of the closer peaks. This would be planned long in advance while we anxiously tried to divine the kind of weather we might expect for our hike. To get an early start, we would spend the night at Aunt Erna's in Füssen, right at the foot of the first range, and start climbing after breakfast. It was a wonderful feeling to reach the top and look down into the green and wooded plains. We were all, locals and newcomers alike, grateful to live in such a beautiful land-scape and felt superior to and slightly disdainful of the flatlanders.

Another favorite excursion was a visit to *Schloss Neuschwanstein,* the weirdest of crazy King Ludwig's castles, also a good hike from the little town of Füssen. King Ludwig, handsome but melancholic, would bankrupt himself building but not finishing this most showy of German castles. His short life ended with his and his private physician's death by drowning in nearby Lake Starnberg. Little did we know that this castle, which on a fine day we could see from our own yard, had been the hiding place of Hitler and his inner circle. There were thousands of pieces of looted art stolen from museums in all the German-occupied countries and from the families of rich Jews. As close as we lived, I never heard mention of that fact, or of the Amer-ican military tackling the huge task of identifying and finding the rightful owners and, as far as possible, returning these treasures to them.

A sad and difficult episode interrupted my mostly happy child-hood. My mother suffered a hernia, probably from heavy lifting, maybe while pulling buckets of water out of our well. We had tap water, which must have been pumped out of the creek that ran at the bottom of the hill on which the hamlet was clustered, the same creek in which we bathed during the summer. But the quality of the water was poor in the summer. The well water was much fresher and tasted so much better. Eventually, my mother had to face the fact that she needed an operation. There was no one to take care of us during the ten or so days she would have to stay in the hospital. In the end, we were placed in an orphanage run by an order of nuns. I was one of the older children there and, thanks to my skills with the sewing needle, I was allowed to stay up late with the nuns in the evening, darning children's socks and mending torn clothes. I visited my mother in the hospital after school and I was glad when she was finally dismissed and was able to take Micky and me home again to our little room. I am still sad when I think about the children who had no prospect of leaving the orphanage until they were young adults. What would be their fates? I happened to be in Pfronten, where the orphanage was located, on an excursion a year or so later. My stay at the orphanage had made a lasting impact on me, and I stopped in to say hello to the sisters. They remembered me but they had bad news. Sister Emeran, the senior nun at the time of my stay, had just died and lay in state waiting to be buried. She looked so peaceful, as though she were sleeping, surrounded by flowers and burning candles. She was the first dead person I had seen in my life. I sprinkled her with holy water and said my goodbye.

Even though my mother never told me so, I know now and dimly knew then that along with the hernia operation, she also had an abortion. As an adolescent and well into adulthood, I struggled with hostile feelings toward my mother about this. I believe in a woman's right to choose, but I was angry that she let herself get into such a situation. Life has beaten some of my self-righteousness out of me, and today I feel great sadness for the anguish she had to have suffered, arriving at this painful decision. She loved children and would, years later, sometimes wistfully say that we would all have loved a third child if there had ever been one. No doubt, there was pressure from the father, the cheesemaker, whose reputation and career would likely have been ruined. Maybe she was still married to my father at that time and feared the consequences. I doubt that she confided with anyone in the village. Aunt Erna, her only close friend, now lived a train trip away. Telephoning was not an option. Only the Settele family in the village had a phone. It was available to all for emergencies only and afforded no privacy. It had to have been Aunt Erna who located a doctor and hospital where my mother could be helped.

Edeltraud Hildegard Widawski, the author's mother, holds her newborn daughter, Sept. 2, 1937.

The author's father, George Janiel

Left: Author's parents' wedding, 1932.

The author's mother, author age 6, and baby brother, Micky, born 1942.

Aunt Enra, author, Aunt Mimi, and baby Micky.

The author in the park with brother Micky.

Uncle Hansi, 18, says goodbye to author after being drafted in 1941.

Author and her mother in front of the house in Enisried

Author at age 12

The house in Enisried in which the author and her family lived in one room for five years

The author, 21, in Istanbul

The author as the young wife of an American

The author married Terence Grieder, a professor at the University of Texas.

The author and her children visit family in Germany, 1964

Christmas 1972

Visiting the old home in Enisried

Ghana, Togo, and Benin, 2021

In Oaxaca, Mexico, for the Day of the Dead, 2023

4. Getting educated

When I turned ten, having completed the fourth grade, I passed the entrance exam for what we called *Oberschule*. At that time, and maybe still today, German children who aspire to a university education, or rather, the children whose parents aspire to such an education for them, are split away from the ones who will follow a vocational path. My mother's boyfriend loaded both my mother and me onto his motorcycle and took us to a near town where I would take the entrance exam in a convent school. For a while, it was even considered that I should board there if I were accepted. Even though I had a good deal less than four full years of school behind me, I did well in that exam. The writing component was to retell a story that had been read to us. That was the first time I heard the story of young George Washington cutting down the cherry tree. It was to my advantage that I had a lot of experience in the retelling of stories. Sharing a room with the two older farm girls and having little entertainment in the hamlet, we had made an agreement that any one of us who had the chance to see a movie would tell it to the others lying in our beds in the dark room.

I started to attend my new school not as a boarder with the nuns but as a day student in Füssen. I went there by train every day, making new friends that came from other little villages along the route. The most exciting new adventure was to start learning English, my favorite class. This gave me a new feeling of empowerment. Back home from school again in the afternoon, I still hung out with my old friends from the village, but we all understood that something now separated us. I was learning something that no one in the village knew, not even my mother or Aunt Erna.

Even though the distance was only about thirty miles, the trip to Füssen took more than half an hour because it was what we called a milk train, stopping about six times before our destination. Here was a new circle of friends for me. At every stop a few more kids would get on, also going to my school, and they were all refugee kids. I got to know them, but I was not immediately accepted. Eventually they got tired of bullying me. Now they were picking on other newer kids, and to my shame, even though I did not participate in their nastiness, neither did I speak up. Classes started at 8 a.m. The walk to the train station was easily a mile, which meant that I had to leave the house very early, in pitch darkness during wintertime. I was small, and as usual, ended up getting a seat in the first row. Because I sat up front, I, likely the least religious of us all, was appointed to speak the daily prayer to start the day. It was a progressive prayer, no mention of God, let alone Jesus, just "Creator Spirit." I remember taking liberties and was never criticized. If I wanted to burn time, I added "In the name of the Father, and the Son and the Holy Spirit," sometimes even twice, at the beginning and the end.

In the morning, the train connection to school was just right; the afternoon return home not so. There was a wait of more than an hour. We would hang around the train station where the city had done a little landscaping and had placed a few benches. One day another girl and I were sitting on such a bench, when a local man in *Lederhosen* (Bavarian leather pants) sat down at the other end. Men were as likely to wear *Lederhosen* as boys. They fit loosely and are worn with their own suspenders, trimmed out with white felt and green accents and maybe even a nice carving of a stag in a rosette made of the base of a stag's antler. In front these pants have a flap, which is buttoned to the waist. The man wore such pants and he had arranged the flap in such a way that he created a gap behind it. In this space, he was displaying his genitals for us to see. None of us was prepared for this, and none smart enough to alert police. Instead, we went around and told each other what we had seen and one after another of us sat on the bench to see for ourselves.

The train station soon got boring. We explored deeper into town and found a tiny chapel, unattended but unlocked, which held skeletal human remains. Like most kids, we were intrigued by the macabre. For the following days we went back to the little chapel as soon as classes were over. Apparently, it was also visited by others, who must have noticed that the bones were now arranged differently. One day we found the door locked, and it would remain so from then on. Another place we sometimes visited was known as the *Mang Fall*, a picturesque waterfall where the river Lech breaks out from between huge boulders with a lot of rushing water, noise, and spray on its way to join the waters of the Danube. There is a rock with a large indentation in the shape of a foot, where St. Magnus (Mang) is said to have jumped across the Lech when he was pursued by enemies of his Christian faith.

It was in the summer of 1948, under the guidance of the Allied Forces, that the democratic German government reformed the currency and created the new German Mark. Every person in West Germany was issued forty marks in freshly printed, crisp bills. Even coins came in the form of small-sized paper money. For one day only, it seemed that all inequalities had been removed and we were all the same, local or refugee, rich or poor, depending on one's outlook. This was also the end of rationing and the beginning of abundance on the store shelves. From that day on, my mother insisted on paying ten marks as monthly rent for our room. As Germany rebuilt its industry, the determination and hard-working habits of its people, with help from the United States in the form of the Marshall Plan, brought about what was to become known as the German "Economic Miracle." The *DMark* became one of the most powerful currencies in the world until, as the Euro, it was folded, some thirty-five years later, into the currency basket of the newly formed European Union. What Hitler had aspired to and failed to accomplish, cooperation and enlightened self-interest would achieve. Europe became unified.

I was about thirteen years old when everything about our lives changed again. The Dairy Farmers Cooperative transferred my mother's boyfriend to a distant location, possibly to put an end to his somewhat scandalous relationship with a married, later divorced, refugee woman, a mother of two. Little by little, some of the refugee families moved away as they found real work and real lodging. One or the other young refugee married a local person and would stay forever. It was almost five years after our arrival on the back of a flatbed trailer pulled by a tractor that we, too, moved away. Aunt Erna had leased a new movie theater in Speyer, a beautiful little medieval town in the upper Rhine valley, not too far from Heidelberg. There was work for my mother, who would sell tickets and keep the books, and a real apartment with modern plumbing was waiting for us to live in. A much more ordinary life began for us children.

Getting Micky into his school was seamless. He was enrolled in the nearest one, close enough to walk alone after only a couple of days. I found out, the hard way, what it meant to move from one occupied zone to another. Bavaria was part of the American zone; Speyer, where we would live now, was in the French Zone. Even the Western allies, who would remain friends, acted proprietarily in the regions they had been awarded in the great bargaining after war's end. And what is the easiest way to establish a lasting bond between occupiers and occupied? By establishing a shared culture, and if you cannot share history, you can at least speak the same language.

I had started my foreign language studies in American-occupied Füssen, with English from day one. The following year Latin was added, and the next year, in addition, we started to learn French. In Speyer, the first foreign language was French, the second was Latin, the third English. My mother's attitude was, "You are smart, you can figure this out," and I was enrolled in a school in Speyer. That did not work out. They were way ahead of me in French, and I, with three years of English under my belt, was bored by their baby English. The only remedy was to send me to the nearest school in American-occupied territory. That place was Schwetzingen, across the Rhine, only ten miles distant, and there was a bus line. I was already used to commuting to school by train, so the decision was easy. The daily trip back and forth would be much longer than the eighteen minutes estimated today by Google Maps for travel by car. For the first two or three years of the five years in which I would travel to and from school five days a week, all traffic across the Rhine had to be by ferry. The Germans had dynamited their own bridge during the last days of the war in the futile hope that this would stop the Allied army. Eventually a handsome new bridge was built, and my commute was shortened. Later, when I had a spiffy bike all my own, green with saddle bags for books and such, I would often go to school by bike, saving the bus fare, and along a stretch where the road ran on top of a dam along the Rhine, I would practice riding with no hands. I also passed a large field of strawberries. Homeward-bound I sometimes stopped for a handful of stolen berries. In Iran, the fields and the orchards are seldom fenced. Custom and the rule of law say that passersby may sit and rest and eat from the fruit, but they may not take any with them. I think that is an excellent rule.

While this change cost me some joys—my village friends, the view of the Alps, the clean country air, the wholesome food, the woods with their mushrooms and berries—I also gained much. Speyer, though small, offered music, theater, all the movies I wanted to watch in my aunt's theater, and libraries, none of which I had missed because I had not known they existed. I loved going to concerts and plays, but still today remain overwhelmed at libraries. Speyer has a lot of history. It was on one of the main Roman roads and still has a well-preserved Roman tower-gate in the center of downtown. Its greatest pride, the Romanesque cathedral which can be seen from miles away above the Rhine and is one of three in the region, was built around A.D. 1000. This *Dom* is the burial place of several German emperors and has been declared a UNESCO World Heritage Site. Before Hitler, Speyer had a thriving Jewish community. A square is still, or again, called *Judenplatz* (Jewish Square), and ritual baths located within the charming old city can be visited today.

I hate to admit it, the quality of our education was not very good. Most of our teachers were male. Most of them had been drafted into the military and they came back damaged in body or psyche. While our foreign language teachers were knowledgeable and well-intentioned, they were not native speakers, nor had they lived or even traveled in the home country of their subject. Germany had been at war with these countries for six years. When we were seniors, we made a class trip to Strasbourg, now French again, and overnighted in Colmar, where we visited the famous Isenheim Altar with paintings by Matthias Grünewald. We were enchanted by the city and its cathedral, and when, for one semester, we had a young Frenchman at our school to assist us with pronunciation, all the girls had crushes on him. I had my own puppy love affair with a French boy, who was in Speyer to visit his parents when he was on vacation from his school in Avignon. I enjoyed using my growing vocabulary, talking and writing letters. German high schoolers had to, and likely still must, pass an exit exam to get their *Abitur*, similar to a baccalaureate. All my classmates passed, and since I had been commuting from Speyer and now no longer had any reason to go to Schwetzingen, I would not see them again.

What next? Of course, I wanted to go to university, and I knew I wanted to learn modern languages. This is the time where the absence of my father really hurt me. When I asked him for financial help with my studies, he gave me a firm "No." In his opinion, I should look for a nice man and get married. He did not want to give me advice, and giving it was beyond my mother's ken. I applied at the Institute for Foreign Languages, part of the University of Mainz, located near Speyer, and without any counseling available to me, I selected English as my major and Russian as my minor. Not until classes started did I realize how foolish I had been. I was the only one not a recent arrival from the Russian zone. All the others had had eight years of mandatory Russian in public school and were fluent, while I struggled with the Cyrillic alphabet. Going to class was torture; I dropped the course. Now I needed a new minor, and floundering about undecidedly, I took the suggestion of a friend and changed to Turkish. This not so well-thought-out choice had life-changing consequences, and I remain a lifelong learner of Turkish.

I had no money for school. My meager scholarship never paid my fees on time, and I worked too much, mostly waitressing at wine festivals. One day I saw on the Turkish bulletin board that The German School of Istanbul was offering the position of "Assistant to the Director." I applied and, possibly being the only applicant, I got the job. Now I needed to apply for a work visa, and I needed to teach myself typing and shorthand.

Waiting for my visa, I stayed in Munich with my Aunt Erna

and helped in the restaurant of her landlord in exchange for our meals. I loved seeing the urban side of Bavaria and visited all the good museums and churches and parks, and I practiced my typing. I made the trip to Dachau, a humbling experience. Aunt Erna had lost her movie theater in Speyer due to a lack of capital and was trying to launch a business producing frozen potato dumplings. We were constantly fiddling with the recipe and cooking to test the result. This venture never got off the ground, and after she suffered a stroke, she gave up and retired. By that time her brother, Fred, lived in a luxury estate at Lake Starnberg, near Munich (remember, King Ludwig drowned there). He had become a millionaire as a manufacturer of all sorts of bread. There were still many small bakeries but selling his products in supermarkets at a lower-than-bakery price was a winning combination. His trucks bearing their family name "Krohe" were seen all over Munich. I don't think that my aunt ever asked him for financial help. He certainly did not volunteer any. Both my mother and my aunt were convinced, but had no proof, that his start-up working capital came from the sale of my mother's rings, which had disappeared when he had been visiting in Enisried.

5. Coming of Age

Eventually, the Turkish visa and transit visas for Yugoslavia and Greece were issued, and Aunt Erna gave me a rose when she kissed me good-bye at the Munich *Bahnhof* (train station) as I settled into my second-class, hard bench seat on the Orient Express on my way to Istanbul.

It was a long trip, three days and two nights, and not as glamorous as the train in Agatha Christie's *Murder on the Orient Express*. I felt light, as though I had jumped off a cliff and not yet landed. The farther east we traveled, the more fellow travelers brought out baskets of food and offered it around. Traversing Yugoslavia, a young soldier in uniform sat next to me and fell asleep with his head on my shoulder. I would push it away, but he was soon back again. In Greece the conductor, who liked to chat with me, asked "Where are you going?" I said, "Istanbul." "No," he answered, "Constantinople. Come, I'll show you something." I followed him to a car at the end of the train, which was even less comfortable. The benches had been removed, and people of all ages were sitting on the floor or on piles of their belongings. Some were frying potatoes on camp stoves on the floor. He said "These are Turks. Do you really want to go there? Better stay in Greece."

I arrived in Istanbul and as I was going through Immigration, Customs took away my little radio, my only possession beyond my clothes. I was relieved to see a man holding a sign with my name. Herr Kapps turned out to be the official fixer at the school. There I met my new boss, Dr. Robert Tenbrook, in his office. He and his family lived in an apartment on an upper floor of the school. A furnished room had been rented for me only steps away, in the Teutonia German Club, where meals were served in the evening. Madame Ganswind, my host, was the widow of a German aristocrat.

My office was large and pleasant. Visitors for Dr. T. had to go past me to his office, even larger and more beautiful than mine, with a fine large carpet on the floor. Despite my fancy title, I was a secretary and was paid the same salary as a grade-school teacher. The school was for the kids of German expats and select Turks, first grade through *Abitur*. There was a Turkish vice director, and half the faculty of about sixteen were Germans, half Turks. I saw nothing that I did not like or could not manage. Only my typing and shorthand had plenty of room for improvement. My hours were eight to five Monday through Friday and eight to one on Saturday, but there was slack in my schedule to chat with Herr Kapps and the secretaries in the front office, who were a great help for me in getting my bearings. My boss had visitors and went to meetings. Then he had lunch and an afternoon nap, and around 4 p.m. he used to come down and, striding back and forth in my office, dictate without notes until 5 p.m., when he retired, and I could go home. As I glanced at my shorthand notes, I could not read a single word, but I took them home and put them under my pillow. The next morning I would type up what I could decipher or remember, and most often he signed. A few times he asked, "Did I say that?" and I would answer, "Here it is, black on white." My job came with a little prestige. The German Consulate had social events, and I was now on the list. Dr. T. was nice to me. If he went for a haircut at the Four Seasons, he invited me to come along and have a coffee while he was being barbered.

As time went by, he little by little became less formal, and between afternoon dictations he would tell off-color jokes. I agonized over my response: should I laugh, or act as though I did not get it? I was not brave enough to tell him to stop. Later I got acquainted with my predecessor. He had harassed her, too, or they had had an affair. I also learned that he did not get along with his board. In the end, he would leave the school before I did.

I still had in mind that I could study Russian privately and go back to my degree plan. The Russian Embassy was in walking distance, and I went there once, during my lunch break, to ask if they could help me find Russian language lessons. I remember being led to a room without windows, where I waited alone for some time and got scared. I got out safely but was scolded by Herr Kapps, who said that I had been recorded by security cameras going in and out.

My work and my digs were in the heart of Galata in spitting distance from the iconic Genoese tower high above the Golden Horn. That is where Istanbul's Christians, Jews, and other non-Muslim foreigners lived. The streets there are too steep for cars. The sidewalks have steps, and *hamals* (load carriers) walked up and down carrying padded backpacks, held in place with a tumpline, a strap across their foreheads. One of the streets had only stores selling a myriad of musical instruments. A *derwish tekke* (lodge) was the school's neighbor, but because these deviations from Sunni Islam were forbidden then, I never saw any *derwishes*. To avoid the steep climb, one could ride the Tunnel, Europe's oldest subway, only two cars long between only two stations, top and bottom. Below, a bridge crosses the Golden Horn to Sultan Ahmet, the heart of Byzantium, where Hagya Sophia, the Blue Mosque, the

Sunken Cystern, Topkapi castle, the Hippodrome where the chariot races were held, and many other historical monuments all are cheek to jowl. There was so much to explore, but the most exciting place was the Grand Bazaar, built around A.D. 1450, a warren with sixty-one covered streets and about four thousand stalls, mosques, baths and restaurants, some of which were old cara-vanserais—rest houses with accommodations for the camels in the center. Surrounding it on four sides were rooms, often two stories, as sleeping quarters for the traders of the Silk Road. Here you could, and still can, buy genuine and fake antiques, and anything else, especially handwoven carpets. The most revered of the merchants was the last surviving eunuch of the Ottoman court, a wizened, blind little man, as pale as an albino, who sold old lamps made of chiseled brass and waxed linen from the days before elec-tricity. There was a steady stream of young folk who came to pay their respects to him by kissing his hand and then lifting it to touch their forehead.

I made acquaintances among my fellow German expats, and for a while I went out with two young physicians who were friends, one of them half German, the other all Turk. At a dance I met a young American, and—fast forward—we were married, had a baby, and had a second one. That put an end to my exploration of Türkiye beyond a day trip to the beach on the Black Sea coast, where we would swim and picnic, and Bursa, a former capital, where my boss and his wife had invited me along as translator. I spent the weekend seeing historic monuments, riding a taxi up a snowy mountain (a trip for which the driver padded himself with layers of newspaper under his shirt), and bathing in the hot mineral water of the hotel pool.

The first to be born was my daughter, Sharon. The pregnancy had been difficult. I worked until a week before her birth, now commuting by bus from Etiler (Hittites), then a functioning village with views of the Bosporus and shepherds grazing their flocks on the hillsides, today a part of greater Istanbul. Only days before Sharon's arrival, the Turkish military had executed a successful coup and taken the reins of government, with ex-President Menderes and his ministers imprisoned on the islands off the cost of the Sea of Marmara. Menderes would be hanged. A few decades later a new Istanbul airport would be named after him. The country was under a nightly curfew, but my labor was painfully increasing, and after checking in with our neighborhood watchman, we walked to the bus station in hopes of finding a taxi. We had no car. There was no taxi, but a bus was about to take off, despite the curfew. It took us close to the hospital and we walked the last bit. Sharon came into the world around 5 a.m., early, weighing barely five pounds. I was nervous when a week later we left the safety of the hospital with a booklet in Turkish, my only source of information on baby care. A year later, when the second child, Steve, was born, weighing eight pounds, I was more experienced and more confident. Three months after his birth, the US Air Force transferred us to Charleston, S.C. The next five years I focused on raising children, learning the American way of life and how to drive a car. The year was 1961; John F. Kennedy was president. Segregation of the races could not have been more pronounced than there, the very place where the Civil War had begun with the first shots fired at Fort Sumter. Self-righteous, as we Germans are wont to be, I spoke out for equal rights and made myself unpopular. The few times when I had a chance to explore, I used the bus and made a point of sitting as far back as I could, making the white passengers angry and the black ones uncomfortable. I was getting a driving lesson from a neighbor-friend when the radio announced President Kennedy's assassination.

6. Texas

The year was 1967. My kids were six and five years old when my husband was transferred to Austin, Texas, a change in which I had no vote and about which I was not happy. We were living then in Myrtle Beach and had bought a sweet little house in walking distance of the beautiful, sandy beach. When we found a much lesser house in Austin that fit our budget, I enrolled the kids in the nearest school, Sharon in first grade, Steve in kindergarten. It was January and patches of old snow were still left in shady spots. On Day One, Sharon came home to the motel where we were still staying with a note pinned to her sweater. I had dressed her in long pants, and the note said that, according to the school's dress code, girls dressed in pants had to wear a dress or skirt over them. After we were settled in our little house, I started looking for a part-time job that would fill the hours when the kids were in school. As an English major, I did not think that I had much to offer competing with native speakers and was happy to accept part-time employment by Austin National Bank, the largest independent bank in Central Texas and proud of it, at a starting pay of $1.50 per hour. That was what we call the good old days.

My brother gave me his old car. I had a feeling of independence. Three years later the marriage was pronounced dead, and we got a divorce.

Banking was then a male occupation. There were about a dozen white male officers and a herd of female clerks, all white, of whom I was one. I had never considered banking as a career, but I did feel like a duck that had been put into water. I organized my work as the bookkeeping department of our Bergstrom AFB branch, got it done faster. But because it took me less time, I collected a smaller paycheck. I took classes in bank operations and aced them, moved to full-time work, had modest promotions and was transferred to a job in the Congress Avenue headquarters.

In 1972, I married a young professor, Dr. Terence Grieder, teaching art history at the University of Texas. He also had two children. Now we were six around the table. At the same time, both of our careers took off. Terry was a wonderful husband, father, son, teacher, and friend. He was a rising star and well loved by his students. He had started out on the studio side and earned an MFA in painting and sculpture. His first job was to teach fifth graders, and after doing that for two years, he went back to school to earn a PhD in the history of art. His specialization was pre-Colombian art, and he, having been interested in indigenous cultures since boyhood, did research as the primary investigator of three good-sized archaeological projects, the first two in Peru, the last in Ecuador—reason enough for me to take Spanish classes. When he was doing field work, I would take my annual vacation in the country where he was working and spend time at his dig, washing shards and socks in the irrigation ditch or taking day trips exploring the surrounding area. He believed that if he dug it up, he needed to write it up, and he published five scholarly books and one textbook. His South American colleagues said, "Grieder has a good eye," and, indeed, in all three of his own excavations he found loads of interesting cultural material. I was lucky to have him in my life. But the gods were getting jealous. We had been married forty-six years when, in 2018, Terry died peacefully after a long illness.

Austin was becoming a hub for high technology and more active in international commerce. On a long shot, in about 1975, I had submitted an unsolicited proposal to the bank's management to create a department of international banking services that would support importers and exporters. My timing was good. An incubator at UT helped startups to get off the ground. More important, under Affirmative Action, banks had to promote deserving women. I was here, a proven entity and cheap. The bank accepted my proposal, and I built the area. It was grand. I was chosen for a two-year graduate bank management program of Southern Methodist University. It helped that in 1981 we merged with Interfirst Bank Holding Company, which already had a wide net of international correspondent banks and far better infrastructure. But while my own career was blossoming, rough times lay ahead for banks and other financial institutions, such as savings and loan associations and credit unions. Two Texas banks, both on the brink of insolvency, my bank, Interfirst, and a competitor, Republic Bank, merged and became First Republic Bank. It turned out not to be a marriage made in heaven. Soon threatened by insolvency again, we were rescued in 1988 by NCNB, headquartered in North Carolina. The combined new bank became NationsBank. After each merger, I had a counterpart in the other bank, and each time I was the one who survived. Personally, I had started to invest in a couple of residential properties. I had access to credit, and I knew how to use it. The houses had to be small; that was all I could afford, and they had to be close to City Center, so I could show them to prospective tenants during my lunch hour. That turned out to be a good bet. In 1994, when my job went to Houston, I retired early at the rank of vice president.

We all try to leave our mark on this earth, and we do it in many ways: how we send our children into the world, what people will remember about us, what work we have done to improve the world. After the modest first beginnings in owning real property, I became more ambitious. I have rescued nice houses, kept them out of the landfill by moving them to a new site and giving them a new life. I have made houses larger, better, have built them from scratch. I have created a fair number, maybe twenty, good and affordable residences and given tenants the opportunity to become homeowners. I think that, had I had the right advice as a high school senior, I would have become an architect. But I have few regrets. My first love was language, the spoken and written word. At my once-a-month visit with my psychiatrist, I joke that I now forget words in six languages. He calls me the poster child for aging.

Istanbul, where I came of age, was and is my jumping off spot for travel to the Middle East, Africa, Central Asia, the Far East, Southeast Asia. I love to visit Germany and use it as a stop on my way to its European neighbors. I travel to revisit old destinations and explore new ones. There are still white areas on the world map in my head.

My husband, Terry, also liked to travel. When he was nineteen years old and had saved up a little money he had made by baby-sitting and mowing lawns, and with the help of his parents, he booked an ocean crossing to England, and on arrival, bought a bicycle and started a tour of Europe. There he was for his first personal encounter with historic monuments and the cultural treasures in the museums that later he would be teaching to university students. Türkiye was not at the top of his travel list, but he went there with me twice. The first time, we decided to spend all our time in Istanbul, and he offered to make the hotel reservations. I had to pinch myself to believe it: he had booked us into the Pera Palace, the famous hotel where Agatha Christie and her entourage would stay when they came on the Orient Express. The hotel is featured in some of her stories. Built in 1892, located in the center of European Old Istanbul, it was already a hundred years old when we stayed there. The only word I can find to describe it is "grand." The suite where Kemal Pasha Ataturk, the founder of modern Türkiye, used to stay is now a museum and can be visited. One evening during our stay, I washed my hair and when I turned on my American dryer, the lights in our room, and probably beyond, went out.

The second time Terry came with me to Türkiye, we stayed in a small private hotel in the Sultan Ahmet district, the old Byzantine and Islamic center of Istanbul, close to St. Sophia Church, the Blue Mosque, and the Hippodrome, where chariot races had been held, and a score of other important historic monuments. Terry was already ill, suffering from memory loss and confusion, probably Alzheimer's. He would die in 2018. I had brought a friend with us, a retired nurse, who would help me take care of him.

Shortly after our arrival, after a nice morning of sightseeing and a pleasant lunch, he and my friend napped in their respective rooms while I went to the market to change money. I met several friends on the way, and it took quite a while to get back to the hotel. When I did, I found our room empty. Terry was gone. I tried not to panic and asked the maid. She said: "He left with his suitcase." I ran to speak with the hotel's landlord, who also owned a shop in what had once been the horse stables for the Hippodrome races, and told him that we had to contact the police. He said, "Not so fast." Thus, I found out that his little hotel was "black market." So we watched the security film, and it showed Terry stepping out of our room and talking to a couple of young men who were smoking in front of the house next door. After a few minutes a car arrived. Terry got in, and they left. One of the two men was still there, and we questioned him. He did not want to talk because they were running a black-market taxi service. Eventually he told us that they took Terry to the airport. I breathed a sigh of relief. A Turkish friend took me there and we spoke to the administration. They made an announcement but told us it was essentially our job to locate Terry. Since I had his passport, I knew that he could only be in the unsecured part of this huge facility. Splitting up and searching, it did not take us long to find him. He was accompanied by two pretty Turkish Airlines hostesses in uniform and he was as happy to see me as I was to see him. He had been missing for about three or four hours in this city of eighteen-to twenty million inhabitants.

You may remember that even as a small child I was already keen to travel, and my passion did not diminish as I grew older. First came the children, and that informed the kind of trip I could take. Then I was employed, for twenty-six and a half years at the bank alone. Managing my money, I could use some for travel, but I had little free time. Finally, after my retirement I was freer to travel, sometimes with my husband, sometimes with women friends, sometimes alone. People often ask me which country I liked best. Thankfully, I have never had a bad trip, but some were better than others. You may be surprised that one of my best trips was to Iran, traveling alone for the first time, thirty days after the US invaded Iran's neighbor, Iraq. For this trip, I prepared by buying the Lonely Planet guidebook and having many conversations with my late, good friend, Hafez, a UT professor, born and raised in an upper-class Iranian family. Twenty years ago, obtaining an Iranian visa required an authorization, for which only an Iranian tour operator could apply. I arranged that. Since I already knew northeastern Anatolia, I decided that I would enter Iran by land.

After a few days of rest and seeing friends in Istanbul, I began the trip in Erzurum, a sober and conservative city, where I also had friends: two young sisters, schoolgirls whom I had met years earlier, and their parents. I had already been to the Iranian consulate in the morning and had been told to come back later. I wrote this in my journal:

April 28, 2003, continued. Back to the Iranian Consulate. This for some reason seems a lot more sinister now. I hear a woman crying in the background, or am I imagining? After a little wait, the same clerk who so nicely told me this morning that visas for US citizens were free, now tells me that my visa will cost $100, and since the bank is closed at this hour, this must be paid to him in cash. I know better than to argue. I still need to send an e-mail to Iran from an Internet Café, and I must study the bus schedule for tomorrow morning, both difficult and requiring a lot of walking. Worn out, I eat my dinner at the hotel and then go to my room for Turkish news on TV and a beer, bootlegged from Istanbul. At about 8:30 the father of the girls, accompanied by them and their brother, comes to say goodbye and bring gifts, predictably a scarf, which will come in handy in Iran, and prayer beads made from the famous local black amber. Quite a day.

April 29, 2003. The sun wakes me long before my planned 8:00 am get-up. By 9:30 I am at the bus station for my 10:00 am reserved bus. No bus! There will be one at 11:00, or 11:30, *Inshallah!* (God willing). Well, there was a bus at 12:30, and it was the world's slowest EXPRESS. The road goes through the middle of a wide valley, bordered on both sides by mountains, the ones on my right being the higher ones and turning their north face toward me, spectacularly covered with snow. The landscape is completely treeless, save multiple rows of poplars, still bare, which were planted as windbreaks for the occasional settlement. The herds of skinny cows and horses soon give way to flocks of sheep, still fat in their winter wool, like dirty little clouds. The driver, rarely ever breaking 40 mph, uses every trick in the book to delay our arrival in Dogubayazit. As the only woman in the bus, seated next to him, I am the last to get off at the terminal, expecting to find easy transport to Gurbulak on the Iranian border, where Lonely Planet promised lodging. There is one single taxi; several men assure me that there is no other transport. We make a deal, $20 for the 18-mile trip. Of course, there is no lodging. The prudent thing to do is to return to town, which I did, the friendly taxi driver generously giving me a discount for the trip back.

Now lodged in a nice hotel, with a good dinner in my tummy, my Turkish money replenished and a beer on my nightstand, the day does not look like a total waste. Just seeing Mt. Ararat, where Noah's ark is believed to have rested when the flood receded, is worth the trip. Distant from the range of mountains, it rises majestically from the plain just above the town. Though it is said to be shrouded by clouds much of the time, it has been my good luck, today and on a previous visit to see it in all its glory. The road to the border runs alongside its foot, and in the evening light its snowy mass seemed to glow.

April 30, 2003. Of all the borders I have crossed in my life this has been the most troublesome by far. I set my alarm at 6:15 to catch the 7:00 am bus to the border, but travel nerves and the muezzin calling the faithful to prayer around 4:30 a.m., made the alarm unnecessary. When I paid TL2,000,000 (You read it right. Two million Turkish Lire=$1.25) for the ride to the border, I smugly congratulate myself for learning so fast. Türkiye later had a currency reform, chopping off six zeros. To this day, some people still call the Lire "Million." Then it was a long walk from the minibus to the actual Customs & Immigration station. Although it was only 7:45 a.m. there were lots of people milling around. They would not let me get in line but ushered me to the front of the queue, and there I hit a snag that no one could have predicted: No electricity, hence no computers, hence no passport processing. I knew that getting upset would not turn on the lights. So, I accepted the only offered chair, sat down and brought out my book. More minibuses full of men kept arriving and passports piled up on the desk. Hardships were pled in vain. Fights broke out among the men crowding around the windows and door. A little after 9:30 the lights came on, and about 30 minutes later the border was opened for me. A huge gate with chain and padlock was pushed open just enough for me and my little roller case to squeeze through. A short walk and a similar gate was opened on the Iranian side. The Iranian official led me into a room full of waiting people, the women in glittering colors, the kids squealing and pushing each other around. The official and my passport both disappeared.

A few minutes later I was invited into a spacious and well-appointed room, with a large and fine Persian carpet, before a Colonel, who looked like a twin brother of my Austin carpenter, Carl, only this one had short salt and pepper hair and a 3-day stubble. I was invited to sit. We established that my Turkish was better than his English. What was the purpose for my coming to Iran? Was I married? Did I have children? How many? Why was my husband not with me? Well, there was a little problem with my picture in the passport. The lamination was a little worn. Why was there no stamp on my photo, and so on, quite amicably. Tea was served. Every now and then one of his men came in, and smartly clicking his heels before the colonel, whose epaulettes identified him as such, reported or asked a question. I offered him some candy from my stash and showed him my itinerary. He offered to send a fax to my tour operator and then to wait for an answer. I suggested that someone look outside the secure area for a man bearing a sign with my name. They did, and the man was found and brought in, and thus I met Jian, who for the next couple of weeks would be my driver, my guide, my translator, my bodyguard, my dinner companion, my everything. More tea was served. Then, I was sent through a cursory inspection by customs, and my passport was finally stamped, but not before the colonel wrote a little note on a slip of paper, folded it and, like a school-boy, passed it to me. It said in English, "You should extend your visa."

As I look at my journal from twenty years ago, I am charmed

again. But this is not a book about Iran, and I must make choices. I cannot tell you about Yazd, the desert city, birthplace of Zoroastrianism with its eternal fire, its squat towers of silence, where the dead were left to the birds. Nor can I tell you about the roses of Shiraz, and the tombs of beloved poets, not to mention the palaces, mosques and bazaars of Isfahan, or the National Treasure of unbelievable gold and precious jewels, well-guarded in the basement of a sturdy Tehran bank building. On both my visits there, an alarm sounded, the doors closed, and steel bars descended in front of them. Somebody had gotten too close to the goods. But I must limit myself to a couple of places and stories. The following is from my journal.

May 3, 2003, To Isfahan. A long day of driving, partly through salt desert, where not even sheep can survive, then vast fields of wheat to supply the thousands of little bakeries baking delicious flat bread with threads of saffron. Two stops, one for a picnic lunch, the other in Khomeyn to visit the house where Ayatollah Ruhollah Khomeini was born and lived. You would recognize his stern face. Returning after agitating for years from exile, he was the first supreme political and religious leader after the Islamic revolution ended over 2,500 years of dynastic rule.

This multi-story house of many rooms around several courtyards, built with thick walls of mud and straw, the inner walls covered with plaster so fine, it looks burnished, is now a museum and meeting place for clerics. When the caretaker heard that I was American, he gave us an extensive tour of the rooms and stables and then invited us to take tea in his office. Sitting on a fine rug on the floor I listened to Jian who translated, and we left with several books on Ayatollah Khomeini, one for me in pitiful English.

May 7, 2003. After a day in Yazd, we are on the road again. We pass through deserts of sand with occasional villages of crumbling adobe, brick, and concrete. We stop at the second oldest mosque and minaret in Iran, made of adobe. It is still visited for Friday prayers. We buy provisions for a picnic lunch, then pass through some low mountains. The desert is now stony with dry tufts of vegetation. Not a sheep in sight. After barreling along at 40mph, Jian turns off the highway down a tree-lined road. We are now in land that gets some water. To my surprise we are at Pasargadae, Cyrus's tomb, grandiose in its simplicity. On a base of enormous proportions made of huge stones, stands a gabled structure made of even larger ones. Here the king was put to rest, seated on his throne with valuable goods and weapons, all stolen by Alexander the Great. We eat our picnic here. We share the place only with the sunburned guardian, who gratefully accepts some of our fruit. Not much farther, again un-warned by Jian, we are in front of three of Cyrus's palaces, or what is left of them, with huge columns, toppled all but one, and reliefs where once were gates, very romantic. Imagine these ruins in a meadow of wild artichokes, poppies and cornflowers, bees buzzing, and larks rising with song.

May 9, 2003. I cannot do justice to the ruin-site, Persepolis, in a few paragraphs. It is an extensive area on a high plateau, surrounded by the Southern Zagros mountains. Here are the remnants of Darius's palace, temples, altars and promenades, the oldest going back to the 6th century BC, all burned, vandalized and looted by, again, Alexander the Great, motivated by revenge for the destruction of Greek sites by their old enemies, the Persians, and by his need for treasure to pay his soldiers. It took many caravans with beasts of burden to carry it off, all chronicled by Plutarch and other contemporaries. What remains are altars, columns, huge stone gates and bas reliefs depicting, in profile, satraps of 28 regions of the realm, identifiable by their faces, hair, clothes and attributes.

As we walked, we encountered one of many school groups,

this one of high school-aged girls, all kerchiefed, as was I. They recognized me as American and wanted to try out their English, something I can remember well from the time when I was their age. They introduced me to their English teacher, who had a worried look. I took great care to speak to her slowly and clearly. She responded, and her pupils were bursting with pride.

The next encounter was quite different. Near the exit a nomad family had pitched their black goat-hair tent. Instead of camels a truck was parked alongside. I offered the woman in the tent a watermelon, which Jian had instructed me to buy from one of many roadside sellers, especially for this purpose. The men were away with their herds. A hen was sitting on a clutch of eggs on a pile of folded carpets. Several ewes were surrounded by their lambs, the tiniest ones inside the tent. The woman offered us cups of refreshing *dut* a mix of yoghurt and water with a little salt. Although only late mid-morning, it was already hot.

The first time I visited Erzurum it had been to explore the extreme north-east of Türkiye, including a visit to Ani, a huge pasture with the ruins of thirteen Armenian churches and one mosque. Across a little creek is Armenia. There are more ancient Armenian churches in the valleys. As I was walking through Erzurum a boy, maybe ten, who should have been in school, sidled up to me pointing out and explaining various buildings. We talked; maybe I mentioned Armenian Churches. With a very serious expression on his face, he advised me "to never get into a car with more than one man." I paid little attention, and when we came to a carpet shop, I went inside. He followed. I have found that carpet shops are a good source of information, and I like to look at carpets and have on occasion bought one. I mentioned to the owner that I was looking for a guide with a car to go into the mountains to find these churches. He said he had a friend with a car and would call him. The boy rolled his eyes. In a few minutes a yellow car arrived with the icon and name of the City on the side, and the friend, a City worker, offered to be my driver-guide. A little negotiating, and we had a deal. The carpet seller asked if he could come along. The boy rolled his eyes even more. I ventured that he might want to stay at the shop, but he was eager to go. Since he had helped me with the arrangements, it felt churlish not to invite him. The boy shook his head, and I gave him some *bakhshish*. We took off into the mountains. In a little village, the houses of which looked as though they were glued to the steep walls on both sides of the canyon road, the men asked me to wait in the car. They would be back soon. After a little while, they returned, put things into the trunk and one of them laid a big butcher knife on the console between me and the driver. Now I remembered what the boy had said to me. After a while we came to a sweet valley with a meadow full of flowers. They parked the car and spread a carpet on the grass. The driver brought the knife with him. I must admit to feeling slightly queasy. It was a great relief when his friend brought a watermelon from the trunk, and they split it into chunks.

Back to my journal.

> We saw a few churches and beautiful views and had interesting encounters, including the righting of a donkey, which, crossing an almost dry riverbed had fallen from an unbalanced load. My new friends jumped in to help, and it was accomplished without even removing the burden.

Not all travel was for fun and exploration. Some was work. One day, when I was still a banker, a man came to call on me and introduced himself by a name familiar in the Austin banking community. He told me that he, a retired bank executive, and a retired Army officer, a man of color, had founded a little Banking School in Haiti. They were teaching topics such as Bank Operations, Supervisory Skills, Effective Communication, and similar courses, but they were constantly being asked by their clients for education in banking services that would support importing and exporting bank customers. By that time the embargo that Haiti had been under for about fourteen years had been lifted. There had been no imports or exports, and only a few bankers had these special skills.

He did not know that Haiti had been on my bucket list for a long time, and that once my husband and I had planned a trip, invited by the former director of the National Museum of Haitian Art, Gerald Alexis, whom we had come to know when he had been at UT for a graduate degree. That trip had been canceled at the outbreak of one of the recurring periods of political unrest. It had become too dangerous. I told him that I would be happy to try, but that I would need some time to prepare the appropriate curriculum. He kept telling me about comfortable accommodations and good French restaurants, and I kept telling, him, yes, I would like to go.

I went to work on the course materials. My thesis from my bank management studies made a ready handbook. In Haiti, the first bank to buy the training was a young and aggressive one. My class of fourteen included all the top management, and, a nice surprise, the CEO was my friend Gerald's brother-in-law. Word spread, and other banks wanted the class. Over the next few years, I may have gone to Haiti as many as a dozen times. I added a second week of instruction in advanced practices. After work, I usually ate the evening meal with Gerald and his family. Gerald is a great teller of voodoo stories, but I remember best a story, Pia, his wife, who worked for UNICEF, told us once at dinner. When she came to work that morning, one of her staff told her: "Madame Alexis, I brought you a nurse today." When she looked at him blankly, he added. "I tied her to the gate." He had brought her a live chicken as a gift, a white hen with a red comb, which looked to him like a nurse in her white uniform and with a red cross on her cap. Once, on a weekend, Gerald rented a *tap-tap*, a colorfully painted minibus, and with the entire Alexis family and some friends I made a daytrip to Jacmel, famous for its pretty colonial architecture. On the way we stopped at an orphanage, supported by UNICEF, where Pia was known because of her work. We were heartily welcomed, and the kids sang for us, in Creole, translated for me by Pia, in part: "Thank, you UNICEF, for the good toilets we now have."

On most weekends I explored alone. Once I flew to Cap Haitien, with its castle on top of a steep mountain. I ascended it on a little donkey, led by a boy of about ten, who was much too smart for the modest opportunities that likely awaited him. I remember eating my evening meal in a small place near my hotel and having to find my way back in complete darkness. Unprepared without a flashlight, I had to feel my way by running my hand along the walls of the few houses I passed. Electricity is a luxury in Haiti and not available to all and not at all times. On the return flight the tiny plane got caught in a vicious thunderstorm. The door to the cockpit was open, and I could see that the wipers could hardly keep up with the torrential rain. We rose and dropped into air holes, sickeningly. Below us was nothing but rugged mountains with no possible landing place in sight. Everyone on board was praying, including the pilots. We landed safely and, certainly on my part, relievedly.

Haiti is an interesting country, deservedly famous for its art, the only place where a slave rebellion succeeded, perpetually struggling with poverty and hard-hit by hurricanes and earthquakes. Once there, I saw for myself how painful an embargo, a common form of sanctioning nonconforming countries, can be for the population. For my early visits I stayed in a nice hotel in Petionville, much higher and cooler than Port au Prince. A man, old and small of stature, made a meagre living helping guests with luggage and such. He walked me to the restaurants and back on nights when I ate out alone. We talked. His wife had contributed to the family income by sewing. He was proud that their kids had finished high school. During the embargo everything was scarce and therefore expensive. The day came when they had to pawn the sewing machine, and when it was not redeemed within a certain time, it was forfeited, a devastating loss to the family.

Because of political unrest and natural disasters, Haiti was becoming increasingly dangerous. I was packing up for my return home for the last time in my second-floor apartment, where I also had a classroom, when loud yelling and beating on the steel door in the tall concrete wall surrounding the house stopped me cold. A group of people were storming the yard and house. I do not know how many there were. I had thrown myself onto the floor. After some time in the house, they were in the yard again, apparently dragging with them the young grandson of the owner, who was crying *va mourir* or *pas mourir* and more that I could not understand. Eventually the thugs left, to my relief, without the boy. Sometime later there was banging on the door again: *Je suis le doctor.* Apparently, somebody had called for medical help. In the morning, when I said goodbye to the landlady and handed her the keys, I did not ask about the night's event, nor did she volunteer an explanation. My friend, Gerald, later wrote me that the mob had already shot to death the boy's older brother over some drug dispute, and they were after the kid now, but had been fought off or persuaded to leave. The banking school closed. Within a year, Pia, Gerald's wife, was shot in the face by an intruder. She survived but lost an eye. They decided to seek asylum and now live in Canada.

7. Last Home

I don't need to be a psychoanalyst to know that the events of my childhood had a big impact on the adult I would become. While I am not a hoarder, I do have a lot of belongings to make up for the spare childhood I had once we had left our "old home." In Bavaria, I had been coveting what the local kids had, and I liked nothing better than the occasional chance to be invited into another kid's attic. Since I had no chance to travel beyond an excursion into near surroundings, I was always dreaming of faraway places, about which I had read, and the best I could do was to collect stamps. My friends and I all did for a while. We got the occasional letter from our Polish relatives, who were mindfully choosing especially pretty stamps. As a rule, the poorer a country, the more impressive the stamps. If I had doubles, I could trade for old German stamps which the other kids found in old trunks or boxes on faded letters tied into bundles with ribbons. One of the things I would have loved to receive was a lamb baked as local mothers would for their children at Easter. Some ten years ago I mentioned this in conversation, and one of the friends present happened to have a lamb mold that she never used, and she gave it to me. Now I bake Easter lambs to give away every year and I bake not only white ones but also a few black.

Living on a farm, I could not have chickens then, but I can have them now, and I have kept chickens for going on eighteen years. I do not let my hens hatch eggs, but I have a few times bought day-olds and have tricked a broody hen into adopting them. I remember the first time I did that. I had a hen who was insistent that she wanted to be a mom. I was running errands and I thought that there are many needs and wishes in the world which I cannot make come true. Here is a wish I can fulfill with little effort. I called Callahan's, a local feed store, and yes, they had day-old chicks. I picked a few and made a cozy nest for them in a small coop, where I could segregate them from the flock. I gave them water and baby chick feed. In the evening, when birds become subdued, I placed the broody hen with the babies. She became agitated and tried to escape, but I told her that it had been her idea, and I closed the coop and hoped for the best. In the morning, when I opened their coop, anxious about what I would find, the little ones were already hopping on top of the big hen, and she was suffering them, clucking maternally. It is a lot of fun to watch a mother hen teach her brood how to be a proper chicken.

Where there is love, there sometimes is sorrow. I live on the bank of a creek which is a highway for predators of all kinds. I have lost chickens to raccoons and a couple have been mauled by dogs not on a leash. I have been thoughtless. My chickens have a generous run, but they love to have the whole big yard, and for their pleasure and mine, I sometimes let them roam. One day when I did that, the wind blew the gate to their run shut, or I absentmindedly may have closed it. In any case, it was already dark when my tenant above the garage, Kristin, told me that one of her favorites was at her door. I realized what had happened and I knew that the chickens, not able to get into their coop, would find places to roost. We set about finding them before the raccoons would make their rounds. We found them in trees and bushes, on the roof of the coop and under it, in flowerpots. One by one we rounded them up. This is how one learns to be more careful.

Since I left Enisried for good, I have gone back a few times to our little hamlet, the place where I spent the most important years of my childhood. Our physical lives were so narrowly circumscribed by extraordinary events on the world stage, and yet we improvised every aspect of our existence from food to education, transport, entertainment, and spiritual fulfillment. My first visit was as a sixteen- or seventeen-year-old. I cannot even remember the occasion for it. Later, I went there with my own children when they were small, and we visited my mother and other family and friends in Germany. Once, Terry and I spent a night there on our way to Italy. I remember I was driving a used Mercedes with a standard transmission that I had just bought, and I was so excited that I got stuck in a wet meadow. Terry had to get us on the path again. The last time I visited the village was with my mother. She was in her mid-eighties then, about my present age, and for health reasons she could no longer make the long trip to Texas for her annual two-month visit. So I started doing the flights to be with her instead. While she really would have preferred for me to stay with her in her apartment and to let her cook for me my favorite meals and wash and iron my clothes, I wanted to take her on little vacations from her routine, sometimes also taking along Aunt Mimi or one of my mother's friends, or both. For this particular vacation, I tried to arrange some rooms for us with old friends in Enisried, which I learned now had a tourist apartment. I booked it for a week. My mother, who had not been back before, was uncertain about the idea of visiting a place where she had endured such hardships. In the end, she agreed, but on condition that she could invite along a friend of hers. You cannot imagine my surprise when, upon our arrival, we discovered that our vacation rental was the former cheese kitchen. No longer an economically viable enterprise, the

Dairy Co-op had sold it to one of the local farmers, who had attractively remodeled it for tourists. The old grapevine still functioned efficiently, now supported by telephones in every house. The news of our visit spread swiftly, and every day, coming home from some sightseeing outing, we would find invitations from friends and acquaintances tied to our doorknob.

One afternoon, we had coffee and cake at the house of my friend, Wolfgang, the Settele son on whose bicycle's handlebar I had long ago gone to the Roma circus. My mother, as she had in every previous conversation, soon brought up the name of her former lover. My friend said, as she had been told several times before, that he was long retired, had married, and was living in a village nearby. But then he added: "I just saw him this morning. Why don't we give him a call?" Next, I heard my friend say into the receiver, "I have someone visiting here who wants to say hello to you, someone whom you used to know very well." And then he handed the phone to my mother. My mother only had to say "hello" when her old sweetheart recognized her voice after all these years and insisted that we immediately come to his house for a visit. This put an untimely end to our coffee-*klatsch*, but ten horses could not have held my mother. My friend and his wife were good sports about the whole thing.

Rather than giving us directions, Wolfgang offered to take us there. He loaded the two old ladies into his big Mercedes, and I followed in my little rental car. When we got to our destination, I jumped out of my car while my friend was still opening the doors and extracting the two octogenarians from his back seat. An old man appeared at the door in his slippers and baggy sweats. The lenses of his eyeglasses were as thick as the bottoms of old Coke bottles. A few wisps of white hair sprouted from his otherwise bald pate. He strode toward me, obviously mistaking me for my mother. He grabbed me, pulled me to his chest and kissed me, saying, "Oh, Traudel," as he used to call her, "that I get to see you one more time before I die." When I was able to disentangle myself and point out his error, we were all invited into the house, and a bottle of wine was cracked open. Then the reminiscing began. I will say, his wife remained entirely friendly and cheerful throughout the whole visit.

Less than two years after this reunion, both the principal characters in this romantic melodrama were dead. I was able to be with my mother during her last days and to hold her hand while she slipped into the next world. After teaching me so many things that would enable me to cope with some of the challenges and obstacles in my own life, she taught me the perhaps most important lesson of all: how to die with dignity. In the meantime, I continue to work and travel, and I got lucky twice. I have a last new love, a gentle man and wonderful poet, who likes to sing. What comes next? I am cultivating an attitude of thankfulness for what is granted me and of curiosity for what still lies ahead. It won't be so long now, and we shall see.

About the Author

Dagmar Grieder is an American by choice, widow of a genius, mother of four, retired banker, lover of foreign lands and languages, friend of the arts, mover and builder of houses. Now in her ninth decade, she believes that the elders of the tribe have a responsibility to tell the stories of long ago. She lives in Austin, Texas.

Looking for your next book?
We publish the stories you've been waiting to read!

A Member of the Texas Book Consortium

Check out our other titles, including audio books, at
StoneyCreekPublishing.com.

For author book signings, speaking engagements, or other events,
please contact us at info@stoneycreekpublishing.com

Printed in the USA
CPSIA information can be obtained
at www.ICGtesting.com
CBHW070344110424
6613CB00006B/10

9 798987 900291